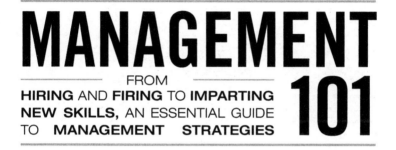

MANAGEMENT

FROM
HIRING AND **FIRING** TO **IMPARTING**
NEW SKILLS, AN ESSENTIAL GUIDE
TO **MANAGEMENT STRATEGIES**

101

STEPHEN SOUNDERING

Avon, Massachusetts

Published by
Adams Media, a division of F+W Media, Inc.
57 Littlefield Street, Avon, MA 02322. U.S.A.
www.adamsmedia.com

Contains material adapted from *The Everything® Managing People Book, 2nd Edition* by Gary
McClain, PhD, and Deborah S. Romaine, copyright © 2007 by F+W Media, Inc., ISBN 10: 1-59869-
143-0, ISBN 13: 978-1-59869-143-6; and *Management Basics, 2nd Edition* by Sandra Gurvis,
copyright © 2008 by F+W Media, Inc., ISBN 10: 1-59869-702-1, ISBN 13: 978-1-59869-702-5.

ISBN 10: 1-5072-0036-6
ISBN 13: 978-1-5072-0036-0
eISBN 10: 1-5072-0037-4
eISBN 13: 978-1-5072-0037-7

Printed in the United States of America.

10 9 8 7 6 5 4 3 2 1

Many of the designations used by manufacturers and sellers to distinguish their products are
claimed as trademarks. Where those designations appear in this book and F+W Media, Inc. was
aware of a trademark claim, the designations have been printed with initial capital letters.

Cover design by Heather McKiel.
Cover images © iStockphoto.com/CSA-Images, song_mi, Robert Wicher.
Interior images © iStockphoto.com.

This book is available at quantity discounts for bulk purchases.
For information, please call 1-800-289-0963.

CONTENTS

INTRODUCTION

Like everything else in the workplace today, the concept of what it means to be a manager is changing. And it's not getting any easier. The workplace has become a complex environment that includes faster and faster communication, swiftly changing economic circumstances, remote workers (sometimes on another continent), and data spitting in all directions. The workforce has changed: It's younger, more technologically savvy, and more diverse in every way. Under these circumstances it's easy for managers to feel overwhelmed. How can anyone "manage" all of this?

Management 101 breaks it down for you in a series of simple, clear entries. Whether you're a new manager or an old hand with plenty of experience, here you'll find useful tips for getting the most out of your employees and yourself.

A manager is responsible for directing a group of employees or a project. This sounds pretty simple, but it's really not. The *Wall Street Journal* cites management guru, the late Peter Drucker, to this effect: A manager sets objectives; organizes; motivates and communicates; measures; and develops people. "While other management experts may use different words and focus on different aspects of these responsibilities," says the *Journal*'s writer, "Mr. Drucker's basic description of the manager's job still holds."

At its heart, good management is all about teamwork. As a manager, your role is to lead other people to accomplish goals that will further the larger goals the company has set. You'll be judged as a manager, to a great extent, by how your team functions and the outcome of your project.

This book will show you how to communicate clearly and effectively, plan for success, execute those plans with precision, and more. Above all, it will help you learn how to manage people and projects to achieve desired results. Great managers know how to inspire their employees, mentor the best of them, and help them move up their career ladders. They know how to tell when a system isn't functioning properly and distinguish that from problems with the people who comprise the system. They know how to resolve conflicts and find the right places for the right team members.

Great management skills are not something you are born with; you have to learn them. *Management 101* will teach you the basics of management—offering examples, both good and bad. These lessons will range from how to recruit and retain great people for your team to turning around counterproductive behavior and conducting effective performance reviews.

It's all here in *Management 101*. So let's get going.

WHAT IS MANAGEMENT?

The Flavors of Organization

Look up the word *manager* on the Internet or in any reference book and you will find many different definitions. They range from the coach of a sporting team to an individual hired to manage a celebrity's business or personal affairs to a computer server that provides the communication link between the systems administrator and affiliated devices on a network. But the most common definition is of someone responsible for directing or organizing a group of employees or a project. In other words, someone like you.

Managers of various organizations and companies come in many "flavors"—they can be directors, group or section leaders, various vice presidents, chief operating officers, even heads of boards of directors. In the truest sense, even the president of the United States is a manager.

According to management expert Bill Warner, despite their varying responsibilities all managers have several things in common: They are leaders, project managers, and coaches who use department resources—both people and equipment—to get the job done. They develop strategies, organize the department, set priorities and make decisions, place and ensure the training of their workers, delegate responsibilities, find solutions, make sure employees have adequate resources to do the job, communicate with department and outside sources, and represent (both internally and externally) and help determine company policy.

Managers also have a number of "soft" duties: establishing and solidifying relationships within and outside of the company; creating and nurturing a positive work environment so people can support each other within the team; and coaching—working with individuals such that they have a clear idea of how they can contribute and thus improve their performance so that they may put forward their best efforts. Managers also serve as mentors, encouraging new talent and advising their employees on their career paths. In addition, they act as a conduit to higher-level management as they report on the progress of their department and other issues that can affect corporate decision-making.

When it comes down to it, managers are responsible for everything in their arena. No matter what you manage or how many people you manage, when it comes to your area of responsibility, the buck stops with you.

THE FUNCTION OF MANAGEMENT: THE 80:20 RULE

Vast amounts of information exist outlining what a manager should and should not do. In fact, there is so much information that it is very difficult to know where to start. And even when you know where to look, no one can learn everything. The principal objective must therefore be to identify those ideas that will produce the bulk of the results—and that is an application of the 80:20 rule.

The 80:20 rule states that you will often find an (approximately) 80:20 ratio between related factors. For example:

- 80 percent of the sales revenue derives from 20 percent of the customers.
- 80 percent of the problems are caused by 20 percent of the people.
- 80 percent of the results come from 20 percent of the activities.

With this in mind, you can begin to understand the importance of focusing on the 20 percent that needs to be attended to at any given moment. Focusing on the 20 percent allows managers to prioritize how they spend their time. Because new managers often lack experience, they typically find that their schedule fills up quickly because they try to do everything. Prioritizing enables the manager to have an impact without spending sixty hours a week in the office.

The 80:20 rule enables you to weed out the problems and concentrate on the areas that need improvement. It will also help you identify strengths within your organization, as well as benchmark high achievers.

FROM "BEING MANAGED" TO MANAGER

In a sense, becoming a manager is like having a child. Before your promotion, you were only responsible for one person: yourself. Now you've got other people to look out for: your employees and team members. The decisions you make will affect them—and their careers.

So how do you make the transition from a good worker who produced solid results—resulting in your promotion—to managing others and achieving the same (or greater) level of success?

The first step is *managing yourself*. This includes obvious areas like staying in shape, eating and sleeping well; being accountable for your actions; doing your best; being a good listener; and other concepts discussed in this book. As a manager, you'll be leading by example, and you will set the tone for your entire department. Your responsibilities include motivating your team members to do the best work possible and shaping the team into a cohesive unit that gets the job done.

So you'll want to set a standard for personal excellence, whether it be through taking additional training (and encouraging your team to do so); learning new skills, such as public speaking (even if you have stage fright); and being positive. The latter is especially important in obtaining cooperation from employees, who must feel that you are loyal and that they can trust you. They also need to be comfortable coming to you with their ideas and sense that you will act upon their feedback and suggestions.

"In most cases being a good boss means hiring talented people and then getting out of their way."

—Tina Fey, *Bossypants*

Employees will do their best when working for someone who they believe in and can turn to. They also expect you to be more than competent in, if not on the cutting edge of, your area of expertise. That said, you also need to recognize your weaknesses and theirs, as well as to define areas of improvement and growth.

UNDERSTANDING THE CORPORATE CULTURE

How Things Are Done

Corporate culture is often defined as "how we do things around here," and it reflects the organization's personality, attitudes, experiences, beliefs, and values. A company is like a living, breathing organism, as individual as a snowflake. If you're going to be a successful manager, it's essential that you understand the culture of your workplace and act according to it rather than against it.

Simple things can often trip up a new manager who is not "schooled" in the cultural norms of the organization. Hazards include who to copy or not to copy on e-mail, when and if to skip links in the chain of command, how to act when you are directly engaged by your boss's boss, the tone to take in written communications and meetings (direct versus political), and how to act at social functions (to drink or not to drink, who to sit with, etc.). These are just a few areas a new manager must understand.

Theories abound that explain corporate culture. Among the most insightful and commonly used is a model from MIT professor Ed Schein, who describes it as existing on three cognitive levels. At the first or "surface" level are the attributes that can be seen by the outside observer—physical layout, dress code, how employees interact with each other, the company's policies and procedures, and organizational structure. The next "middle" level consists of the professed culture of the company: its mission statements, slogans, and stated values. At the third and deepest level are the organization's tacit assumptions, the "unspoken rules" that are rarely consciously acknowledged even by the employees. Here you'll find taboo and sometimes contradictory elements of company culture.

Not only must managers understand all three levels of a culture, but they must also know how to navigate the complex and often-conflicting third level, a task that requires the utmost tact and sensitivity. It is in this third level that managers face their greatest challenge. To ignore or bypass the company's unspoken rules and taboos is to invite trouble and resistance among the ranks and from other managers. The best way to prevent inadvertent slip-ups is to find a peer or manager who can help you understand the more subtle nuances of accepted practices. It also helps to be observant and, especially at first, to become an active listener when offering opinions.

The Four Cultures

It's useful to understand which type of corporate culture you're dealing with. Terrence Deal and Allan Kennedy, in their book *Corporate Cultures*, describe four different kinds of culture:

- Work-hard, play-hard culture (rapid feedback/reward and low risk—restaurants and software companies).
- Tough-guy macho culture (rapid feedback/reward and high risk—police, surgical units, sports).
- Process culture (slow feedback/reward and low risk—banks, insurance companies).
- Bet-the-company culture (slow feedback/reward and high risk—aircraft manufacturers, Internet ventures).

As a manager, you should wholeheartedly support your company's culture, even if you don't agree with parts of it. Change is more easily effected if it's perceived as friendly and coming from within the organization, rather than from an external, potentially hostile force, such as a corporate takeover or outside consultant.

DEFINING YOUR ROLE—GET CLEAR ON WHAT YOU NEED TO DO

Unlike its culture, a company's mission statement is clear-cut. It conveys to the world what the company is about and what it hopes to accomplish. As a manager, you may want to create your own mission statement, even if it's concerning a project or department that you've inherited from someone else. If it's a new venture, then you're faced with the challenge of coming up with something from scratch. First and foremost the mission statement for your organization should reflect and reinforce the mission of the company. Regardless, you might want to work in conjunction with your staff or team to develop the statement so that it reflects the group's ideals.

An effective mission statement should cover the following:

- The department's purpose and objectives
- Its basic philosophy
- How it plans to serve customers, and the community at large
- The department's standards
- How the department will make a difference and fit into the overall scheme of things

Writing an effective mission statement is easier said than done. It should summarize principles and ideals in only a few sentences, as in the following example.

The Ohio State University Wexner Medical Center's Mission, Vision and Values

All areas of our organization are driven by our mission: to improve people's lives through innovation in research, education, and patient care.

We also share a common vision: working as a team, we will shape the future of medicine by creating, disseminating and applying new knowledge, and by personalizing health care to meet the needs of each individual.

Central to how we carry out our mission and vision are our values: integrity, teamwork, innovation, excellence, and leadership.

Source: The Ohio State University Wexner Medical Center © 2007. Used with permission of The Ohio State University Wexner Medical Center.

A solid, well-crafted mission statement will help you clarify your goals as a manager, set forth the department's reason for existence, and establish its objectives.

SETTING UP YOUR MANAGEMENT STYLE

The $100,000 (adjusted for inflation) question facing many beginning managers is this: How should I lead? To begin to answer that question, it's helpful to have a grasp of the most common management styles:

- An *autocratic manager* makes all the decisions, keeping the information and decision-making among the senior management.
- A *paternalistic manager* makes decisions in an authoritarian manner in what he or she perceives is in the best interests of the employees.
- A *democratic manager* allows the employees to participate in decision-making; everything is determined by the majority.
- A *laissez-faire manager* takes a peripheral role, allowing staff members to manage their own arenas of responsibility.

None of these styles is the "right" one. Managers can use any of them. You may be more comfortable with one style, or more commonly, a combination of styles. The right style depends upon the corporate culture or what the situation warrants.

It's also important to understand what drives your employees. Decades ago, the role of management was almost punitive, in that they were to "make" employees do things because they were believed to be inherently lazy and only out for the paycheck. This "old school" of thought, known as Theory X management, was developed by the late Douglas McGregor, a management professor at MIT. According to Theory X, employees are like unruly children, needing close supervision. The manager assigns blame when things go wrong.

McGregor also developed Theory Y management to cover the other end of the spectrum. According to this theory, employees see work as a natural part of their lives. Not only will they accept responsibility, but they actually embrace their physical and mental duties.

Therefore, employees should be given total freedom to perform at the best of their abilities without restrictions or punishment.

Taken at either extreme, both theories have their problems. With Theory X, you have management by fear and intimidation, which is ineffective in eliciting loyalty and long-term results. This style of management limits idea generation since the manager assumes he or she has all the answers and that those answers are always right and best. Theory Y may cause a breakdown in communication because managers hesitate to interfere or hurt employees' feelings. Human nature being what it is, employees may take advantage of Theory Y managers.

Obviously the best management approach is somewhere in the middle, a combination of "tough" and "tender," with an occasional need to go to either extreme. However these models remain useful in figuring out effective approaches to management and in addressing organizational development issues.

MANAGING EXPECTATIONS

What Do You and Your Employees Want?

People work for myriad reasons, but most of these reasons figure into three core factors: They want to be entertained, feel appreciated, and earn money. The job description that covers these needs might read, "Our company offers challenging work, opportunities for career growth, and a comprehensive compensation and benefits package." The excited employee who applies for the position might think, "Finally—a job that will let me use my skills and knowledge in ways that make me happy, a company that will see how good I am and promote me, and a paycheck that will cover payments on a new car!"

The Importance of Social Interaction

Employees often expect their jobs to provide a certain level of social interaction. Going to work is a chance to reconnect with friends and acquaintances. Human beings need this interaction. In most situations, this need is not necessarily incompatible with productivity and efficiency. People work better when they're happy, and interacting with other people is a way to be happy. The challenge for managers is to keep such interactions appropriate for the workplace.

On the surface, an employee's expectations are often brief and clear. He or she wants a reasonable paycheck, reasonable work assignments, reasonable hours, and a reasonable level of respect. The definition of "reasonable," however, is different for each employee and changes over the course of an employee's career. A young, single person at the start of his or her working life might be eager for opportunities to travel and be willing to work long hours to complete complex projects. For a married person with a family, however, travel and overtime might be resented intrusions.

Though expectations vary among individuals, three basic needs are common to most people:

1. To engage in work that is interesting and provides a sense of accomplishment
2. To feel that the job offers economic stability
3. To grow toward personal potential

An employee's expectations begin with the job position posting or advertisement. Someone—hopefully a person who intimately knows the job's technical skill requirements and work environment—attempts to summarize the position's needs in 100 words or less. This can be a considerable challenge, even for the entry-level jobs that individuals might apply for to gain experience. Most job descriptions include a certain amount of "planned ambiguity" to accommodate the rapidly shifting needs of the business world.

Usually, this benefits both the company and the employee. Employers need to be able to change a job to fit new needs. Workers generally appreciate the opportunity to learn new skills and have new experiences. Managers and employees alike who establish rigid expectations based on the job description in place at the time of hiring are likely to resist changes that arise. This can lead to angry confrontations and dissatisfaction on both sides of the management line.

EXPECTATIONS, CLARITY, FEEDBACK, AND FAIRNESS

What do you think your employees expect from you as their manager? Put a check mark in front of the statements you believe are true for you.

My employees expect me to ...

- know what they want, even if they don't say anything.
- understand that they have lives away from work that sometimes interfere with work.
- pick up the slack for them or intercede in some way when they aren't able to get their assigned job tasks completed on time.
- be available at any time of the day to answer questions and resolve problems.
- treat them fairly, which they define as considering any and all extenuating circumstances before passing judgment or taking action.
- help them acquire new skills, even if that means they will then become qualified for different jobs.
- advocate for them when they have needs that require upper management decisions.
- occasionally take them to lunch or bring in goodies as a show of appreciation for the good work they do.
- give them full credit for the department's successes and take full blame for the department's shortcomings.
- always remember that they are only human but to never reveal this about myself.

Most managers will check off seven or eight of these expectations, chuckling over some and groaning over others. Some are not very reasonable or realistic, while others are essential. Some seem selfish—and they are. But all, at some time or another, are valid.

Here's another area of responsibility you may not have considered: While your employees will certainly expect you to advocate for them with regard to upper management decisions, they will also expect you to be attentive to problems that arise between employees. If one employee is causing trouble for the others, you must immerse yourself in the issue until an acceptable solution is reached. Consider the following scenario, for example:

Eve was a brilliant computer programmer. She had the ability to listen to a client's needs, and then produce exactly what the client needed. But Eve wasn't much of a team player. She preferred working alone; she wanted to go away to do her work and return with the finished product.

Eve's department was organized into teams around a structure that encouraged and supported collaboration. When her colleagues confronted her about taking on projects and not telling anyone what she was doing or letting anyone else become involved, Eve swung to the opposite extreme and started delegating everything. She was either on top of her game or at the bottom of the heap—there seemed to be no middle ground.

Responding to complaints from other employees, Eve's manager began documenting the problems. He sat down with her, identified the difficulties, and outlined a way to fix the problems. Eve agreed to the plan, and for a while everything went smoothly. Eve attended staff meetings, presented her projects to her work team, and even seemed eager to work in collaboration with her colleagues.

Unfortunately, the agreement soon broke down. Instead of discussing her ideas, Eve stormed out of meetings. Within weeks, Eve was again at one extreme or the other. Her manager had to make the critical decision of whether to keep her or fire her. The company would sorely suffer to lose her skills (especially if she were to take them to a competitor). But keeping Eve would likely mean losing other employees, and that wasn't a particularly enticing option, either.

Finally, after consulting with the company's executives, Eve's manager offered Eve the opportunity to work from home. She received specific assignments and deadlines, and the manager and Eve's colleagues worked out a foolproof system for staying in close communication. Eve came in to the office periodically, usually to meet with clients, and it turned out to be the perfect solution. Eve was happy, the company was happy, the work group was happy, and the clients were happy.

There had never been any issues around the quality of Eve's work, just around her style of working. Innovative thinking and the willingness to try something different salvaged a highly productive and talented employee, giving the company a strong competitive edge in its market. At the same time, Eve's manager paid attention to the concerns of the other employees. It was a win for everyone.

This incident shows the value of treating employees as individuals. People come in all shapes and sizes—especially in today's diverse workforce. It's important not to try to cram someone into a place in the organization where she just doesn't fit. In Eve's case, her manager found a solution that fitted her and benefited the company.

Start by determining what expectations your employees have of you. Don't assume all these expectations will be the same; they'll vary from person to person. Then review your own expectations—again, these may not be the same from person to person.

COACHING

Bringing Out the Best in Others

Odds are, you remember a coach from somewhere in your past. Perhaps it was a track coach who pushed you to run faster or jump farther than you thought was possible, or a swim coach who pushed you to the edge of your endurance. Good memories or bad, these are powerful reminders that a single person can have lasting influence in the lives of many others.

As a manager you must focus on the needs and capabilities of each individual on your team. Like a coach, you must bring people of diverse skill levels and backgrounds together to work as a unified team in such a way that the synergy among them generates a product or result that surpasses each individual's abilities. Sounds like a tall order? It is! But it's really nothing more than providing ongoing reinforcement of what employees are doing and learning.

An effective coach does a lot of things:

- Provides timely and specific feedback. "Good job!" feels good but says little; "You really nailed the point in your proposal!" lets an employee know what was good.
- Establishes standards and goals that are high enough to make employees stretch, but not so high that they're impossible to reach.
- Tells the truth with kindness and caring—but still tells the truth.
- Shares ideas and offers suggestions but resists telling employees how to do things.
- Teaches people how to cook rather than taking them out to dinner, metaphorically speaking.

- Helps people look at problems from a new vantage point so that they may understand challenges within the context of the entire company and not just their part of it.
- Holds employees accountable for their commitments and goals.

Good coaches inspire loyalty and respect, characteristics that are increasingly rare in the workplace. How do you become a good coach? The most effective way is to watch a good coach in action. If you feel that your workplace is deplorably lacking in such role models, attend some high school or college athletic events. You'll see good coaches, bad coaches, and mediocre coaches, and you'll see how their teams respond to their methods.

The Rise of Consultants

It hasn't taken long for the business world to adapt the concepts of coaching for use in the employment environment. Thousands of consultants offer business coaching services that target the motivation of work groups and individuals so as to improve efficiency and increase productivity. Business coaches charge anywhere from several hundred to several thousand dollars a day for their services. How do you know if they're worth it? Ask around, and check references.

MENTOR

Trusted Guide

Although we view mentoring as a modern concept, the original Mentor debuted in Homer's classic of Greek mythology, *The Odyssey*. When Odysseus goes off to war, he appoints his close friend Mentor to look after his family and household, including his son Telemachus and wife Penelope. When Odysseus is imprisoned, the goddess Athena takes over Mentor's body to guide Telemachus in safeguarding his mother from the actions of greedy suitors who are chasing his father's riches. When Odysseus finally returns home after twenty years, Mentor helps him devise the "test" by which Odysseus proves to Penelope that he is, indeed, her long-missing husband. Mentor also makes appearances in other Greek myths, often as the disguise for a helpful god or goddess.

Today's mentors are ordinary people who have achieved extraordinary success helping others reach their goals. Most mentoring is unofficial, though some corporations have structured mentoring programs to groom potential upper-level managers and executives. More typically, a person with expertise takes interest in a subordinate's career and takes that subordinate under his or her wing. A mentor helps an employee:

- Set long-term goals and short-term objectives
- Explore new directions to achieve goals
- Identify personal strengths and weaknesses
- Find ways to develop and grow

One of the most effective methods of mentoring is shadowing. You put your employee in situations where he or she can observe your actions, or those of others, without participating in them. Your employee might sit in on a conference call or a sales meeting, for example, or read and discuss a report you've written, or accompany you to an event where you are giving a presentation. These lessons are far more effective than any explanations you can offer. Not only do they let your employee see the master in action, but they also show that the master is still human. If you're exceptionally good at what you do, it's because you learn from your mistakes as well as your successes. The better you are, the smaller the increments of measurement. These are subtleties that are difficult to convey in any other way.

"Tell Them What to Do"

Consider this valuable bit of advice offered by General George S. Patton of the U.S. Army: "Never tell people how to do things. Tell them what to do and they will surprise you with their ingenuity."

Mentoring extends beyond teaching in that it relies on establishing a relatively long-term relationship that revolves around sharing and mutual respect. A mentor shares knowledge as well as wisdom—a fine line, perhaps, but a crucial distinction. While knowledge can be learned, wisdom must be acquired. Knowledge is having the right words; wisdom is knowing when and how to say them—and when to keep them to yourself.

TEACHER

Imparting New Skills

A teacher is someone with expert skills and knowledge who has the ability to share this expertise with others. A good teacher improves both the individual student and the company. But it isn't always easy for a teacher-manager to find a balance between "Let me show you" and "Get out of the way, I'll do it myself!"

A small software company hired Miguel to do its PR. The company chose Miguel because he was good at explaining technical concepts to nontechnical people. But Miguel had never used his skills to write marketing materials, and his debut in his new job was less than spectacular. In fact, it was a bit of a dismal spectacle.

After bleeding all over Miguel's first few attempts with her red pen, Miguel's manager called him into her office. For the rest of the afternoon, she became his journalism teacher. She explained and demonstrated the basic principles of journalism. She showed him how to establish those principles—who, what, where, when, and why—in the first paragraph of virtually anything he might write. She showed him how to make up quotes that would pass muster with corporate executives, how to put words in their mouths that they would wish they had actually said (and would say, after reading the stories generated by the press release).

Now, Miguel's manager could just as easily have reamed him out. After all, Miguel had been hired to write press releases, and he wasn't doing a very good job of it. Miguel's manager could have counseled him for his unacceptable job performance and placed a memo in his personnel file.

But she didn't. She put on her teacher hat and turned her office into a classroom. She not only showed Miguel just what she wanted him to do, she also taught him the skills he needed to apply the same lesson to other situations. For a few weeks after, Miguel's manager met with him to strategize the approach for each new press release. Miguel went to his desk to do the writing, then sat down with his manager to review the results. Within a few months, Miguel was getting compliments from senior executives. Not only did Miguel's skill level improve tremendously, but his self-confidence grew as well. He even enrolled in an evening continuing education class at a local community college to further hone his writing skills.

"Good management consists in showing average people how to do the work of superior people."

—John D. Rockefeller, American oil tycoon

Not all situations end in such success, of course. Some people resist the suggestion that they need to clean up rusty skills or learn new ones. Some managers lose patience when improvements fail to be immediate and dramatic. Some managers know what they want from their employees but don't know how to express their needs in ways their employees understand. If the teaching hat doesn't fit you very well, consider alternatives (as your budget allows):

- Hire consultants to conduct workshops or seminars for your work group or department.

- Send employees to training courses (all expenses paid, of course).
- Reimburse or otherwise compensate employees for taking classes that directly improve their job skills.

PARENT

Many people view the workplace as an alternate home and the people there as surrogate family members. After all, you spend more waking hours at work than at home or anywhere else. Coworkers are pseudo-siblings or pseudo-spouses. And managers become—you guessed it—pseudo-parents.

Creating Boundaries

Just as parents need to set limits and structure for their children at home, managers need to establish boundaries and organizational frameworks for their employees at work. As a manager, it is your job to tell employees what they can and cannot do. You—and they—don't have to view this as overly restrictive. Rather, it's the way you get them to focus on the job at hand.

Just as you might have to tell your ten-year-old son to stop spitting out the car window, you might need to tell a thirty-two-year-old administrative assistant that she can't swear on the telephone or a fifty-year-old sales representative that he can't shave during the morning staff meeting. Taking the time to call out behaviors like these may seem petty and counterproductive—and sometimes it is. But people push limits just to be sure those limits are still in place. Everyone needs to feel there's a certain level of stability in their lives, and by setting limits you provide your employees with that stability.

In the role of manager-parent, you will often train your employees in basic behaviors. This differs from teaching them skills. You might find yourself repeatedly reminding employees to ask clients if there is anything else they can do for them before rushing to the next call, just as at home you might find yourself repeatedly reminding your kids to unball their socks before putting them in the laundry basket. Further, your manager-parent role might frequently compel you to reinforce core values and the behaviors that support them, such as prioritizing client requests even when doing so requires interrupting other work.

Sometimes being parental also means providing a listening ear. It might mean dealing with complaints, even some whining, while listening between the lines to understand the real issues. And sometimes wearing your parent hat means being firm and saying, "Yes, I understand this is a lot to do."

Is the Relationship Good?

A 2016 article on the website About.com Money (www.thebalance.com) suggested that respect ranks at the top of the list of what employees want in their jobs: "Part of that respect is praise and feedback so people know how they are doing at work." The relationship employees have with their managers is a key factor in whether employees stay or leave.

When you are functioning effectively in your manager-as-parent role, your employees can be expected to do the following:

- Know and follow established guidelines and procedures
- Understand that there are clear and consistent consequences for stepping outside the boundaries
- Accept accountability for meeting project timelines rather than pointing the finger of blame at others if things go wrong

- Be comfortable in coming to you with problems or concerns
- Respect you, but not fear you

Remember, though, that you are not, of course, really a parent to your employees, and the work group is not really a family. There are important differences, many of which are based on performance. Your employees are adults, and they have adult rights and responsibilities. It does not serve them well, in the long run, for you to make decisions for them as you might for your children. They have been hired to perform specific tasks and accomplish particular goals. You might be wearing your parent hat too long if any of these things occur:

- You look at the employees sitting in your office airing yet another dispute and realize that if they were younger and shorter, they'd be tattling.
- "Nobody told me I had to do that" is a familiar chorus in staff meetings.
- Employees ask permission to go to the restroom or take a break.
- No assignment gets completed without repeated visits to your office to be sure it's being done right.
- You make excuses to your superiors when your employees fail to complete projects either on time or correctly.

FINDING BALANCE

One of the areas in which you'll find yourself exercising your parental role is in finding a balance between people and between different tasks. Acting as a mediator is familiar territory for many managers who feel that all they do is help people find common ground. You might help employees resolve disagreements among themselves, investigate disputes between clients and employees, or negotiate differences between the priorities of upper management and the needs of employees.

Mediation is most effective (and successful) when it is a process of collaboration rather than compromise. This is more than just word play. "Collaboration" comes from the Latin *collaborare*, meaning "to labor together." "Compromise," despite its core word "promise," implies giving up something of value, or conceding a cherished point, to reach agreement. These implications are important because they set the tone for the discussion. Few people are happy when compromise means they get less than they hoped for or expected, yet most are pleasantly surprised to get more.

Mediation is most effective when you aim to do the following:

- Focus on common goals and look for common ground to help you reach those goals
- Treat all parties, and their viewpoints, with respect
- Propose win-win solutions
- Remain interested but impartial
- Establish a process for assessing the success of the agreed-upon solutions

If you act as a successful mediator, over time you'll find your employees create that balance themselves, and you're required less and less to intervene in order to mediate.

CHEERLEADER

Rallying the Troops

People worry about their jobs and their abilities to complete new tasks and assignments. They need someone (you) to rally them back to believing in themselves. As a manager, a major part of your job is to motivate and excite your employees. Leading the cheering section demonstrates that you believe in your team and its ability to succeed. But you have to have those pom-poms always at the ready. It's not acceptable to sit in your office all week, and then pop out when a productivity report tells you that your department is in jeopardy of missing its deadlines. Cheering on the troops is only effective when the troops know that you truly care—not just about their projects and assignments and meeting your department's goals, but also about them as people and individuals. And they won't know you truly care unless you're involved in what's going on every day.

Owning the Process

Many employees resist efforts to make them "better" workers if they perceive that nothing is changing within their work environments to support the "new employee" that upper management wants to see. When companies begin involving employees in identifying problems and designing solutions, there is a dramatic leap in buy-in. Once employees feel they are owners in the process of improvement, they become enthusiastic supporters of improvement efforts.

Do you watch sporting events? Do you watch the cheerleaders? (It's okay, you can admit it.) They're always interacting with the crowd, no matter what's happening on the field or the court. They're chanting and dancing and smiling, working to stay engaged with the spectators. Their mission is to create a roar of support beyond what they themselves can generate, support that motivates the players to give the proverbial 110 percent. But the players know that the cheerleaders are always there. And they know that even when the crowd boos, the cheerleaders are still there, cheering.

This is your role, too. Even when your superiors—or your clients or customers—are unhappy with your team's work and productivity, you need to stay right there on the sidelines, cheering your team on. If you've been there all along, they will respond.

THE NEED FOR STRUCTURE

Finding the Balance

Not all people, no matter how creative, function well in an environment with minimal structure. Some people don't know how to channel their energy into productive tasks with measurable outcomes. Other people crave—and excel under—close and specific direction. Occasionally you'll encounter a person who must have external structure because without it he or she simply won't do any work at all.

Employees who need a lot of structure need a manager who is willing to be more hands-on. Structured people tend to have the following characteristics:

- They are often tidy and organized. Their desks and workspaces are neat and functional. Nearly anyone could step into a structured person's environment and find a file or project.
- They arrive and leave on time, and at the same time every day. If they are early, which many tend to be, they are consistently early.
- They follow obvious routines. Other employees almost always know where they are and what they are doing, just by knowing what time or day it is.
- They know what work is due and where in the process the work is, and they deliver on time unless circumstances beyond their control intervene.
- They handle complex projects by breaking them into smaller, logical steps. Structured people often keep status and progress logs of their projects.
- They appear disciplined and goal-oriented.
- They seldom knowingly break rules, and they might take offense with those who do.

Every company, regardless of its products and services, requires a certain amount of structure. Some functions and departments, such as accounting, are bound to established procedures for conducting their work. People who work in these areas generally (but not always) have work styles and personalities that are compatible with this level of structure. Other functions and departments require structure that supports project timelines and productivity targets. Such structure might require you to precisely establish priorities, goals, and tasks.

STRUCTURED JOBS

The backbone of structure is clear communication. Employees need to know what they are expected to do and by when. What is more important? What is less important? What happens when tasks compete for people, time, and resources? Some people are good at establishing priorities, while others struggle. Sometimes employees have trouble prioritizing because they are unfamiliar with the department, the company, or the industry. They have no context for the work they do, so they don't know what to tackle first. *Everything* becomes critical in such an environment. As a consequence what gets completed is often frustratingly trivial, and the important stuff gets left undone or is missed completely.

As a manager, your role is to help employees who need structure establish priorities and processes to support them. Once the base structure of priorities is in place, most employees can then build additional structure around those priorities. Generally it's most effective to meet with employees one-on-one, so you can gauge just how much structure each employee needs.

Start by laying out specific tasks and the small goals that must be accomplished by the end of the day. Be sure the employee has the necessary tools to complete the tasks and knows how to use them. Next, identify common problems that might arise, and establish a procedure for dealing with them. Some employees find it useful to have a chart or diagram that outlines priorities and procedures, while others might just take notes.

Schedule a follow-up meeting with the employee to discuss how he or she approached the tasks and what actually got finished. Communication about expectations, and what worked and didn't work, is critical here. Establish procedures for identifying and addressing emergencies and unexpected changes in priorities. At first, this might mean having the employee come to you whenever work deviates from the planned schedule. As the employee becomes more skilled in structuring and adjusting priorities, the procedures might shift to general guidelines for when to contact you and when to proceed without assistance.

ADAPT AND GROW

Be willing to revise and adapt. People grow and their needs change, and it's essential to keep up with both. What an employee self-monitors and what you monitor should evolve over time so that you as manager play a less direct role in sculpting the employee's daily activities.

Over time, and as the employee's comfort with the structure progresses, designate daily tasks as part of the employee's routine, with the employee responsible for making them part of the workweek with less monitoring from you. Schedule brief but regular meetings or other processes to provide feedback and reinforcement. You might stop by the person's desk every Tuesday at 3 P.M., have employees generate daily or weekly progress reports, or hold staff meetings.

WORK OVERLOAD

Sometimes an employee's apparent inability to complete job tasks reflects an overwhelming workload rather than a structure problem. In such situations you might need to reassign job tasks to lighten the load. This could mean realigning work responsibilities among your current employees, hiring temporary employees to help out, or creating new positions to accommodate a growing workload.

Each employee has a slightly different need for structure. It's important for you as the manager to remain in close contact with all employees so that you can adjust various elements of structure to support their highest levels of productivity. Asking each employee how he or she feels is the most effective way to structure the workday. By tailoring structure to each of your employees, you help them buy into the process. They feel an investment in it because they helped create it.

CONSISTENCY IS THE KEY

Building Trust in the Workplace

In the workplace, it's all about consistency. If you're not consistent in your practices, employees won't trust you—or each other. One way to make sure everyone is on the same page is to distribute documents that outline the company's policies and guidelines. If your company doesn't have such documents already, don't just leap to your keyboard to begin writing your own policies. Talk with your superiors first. A written policy, even something you send out as an e-mail or a memo, represents your company. Its content can have legal ramifications. Many companies even have policies that outline the process for writing new or revising existing policies and procedures.

It's not very glamorous, but in the end, consistency scores big points with employees because it shapes as well as supports their expectations.

Larisse was a manager for a company that gave bonuses for completed projects. When the company first implemented the policy, the procedure was simple: Each employee had one project at a time, and each project had a timeline. Each time the employee met the timeline, he or she received a bonus.

The company grew and its market became more sophisticated. Projects became increasingly complex, and employees often handled several projects at the same time. To meet timelines, employees started working together, collaborating and cooperating to finish projects. A manager's dream come true, right? Only until bonuses were due, and then it turned into a nightmare. At first, the company tried splitting bonuses among the various employees who worked on the project. This worked only until employees began complaining that two of them did most of the work, while the others made only token contributions.

Because there was no formal company policy about shared bonuses, Larisse became a frazzled wreck. There was no way she could be consistent because there was no structure to support her judgments and decisions. Employees began to feel that she was fickle and arbitrary, even though she often spent hours poring over project time logs to determine which employees had made what contributions.

Though the last thing Larisse wanted was yet another set of rules, she finally felt compelled to ask her superiors for a more comprehensive policy. Within a month she—and every employee—received a copy of the new, detailed guidelines for bonus payments. There was the usual grumbling as everyone dissected the new policy. Even Larisse found a few guidelines that she thought were unfair. But she enforced the policy anyway, because as a manager that was her job. In the end, that consistency restored peace and productivity. And Larisse found great peace of mind, because she no longer had to remember how she had handled a bonus on a previous project and try to figure out if this project had a similar set of circumstances.

Consistency is crucial not only because it establishes standardized procedures but because it also affirms fairness. Even if employees (or managers) disagree with human resources (HR) policies or department procedures, they will accept them when they know everyone else must, too.

THE IMPORTANCE OF LISTENING

Be an Active Listener

The communication cycle alternates between talking and listening. The exchanges are sometimes lengthy, sometimes rapid-fire. It's a back-and-forth process, with each participant playing both roles. Too many people view listening as a passive act when it's actually just as active as talking. The problem is that we tend to spend listening time thinking about what we're going to say next. Or our minds wander and we begin to think about what to cook for dinner tonight, whether those concert tickets are still available, when the cat's due for her next set of shots—anything but what the other person is saying.

Find the Right Body Language

A closed posture implies a closed mind. Folding your arms across your chest and crossing your legs is a classic defensive posture that delivers the message, "Don't mess with me." Rarely is this a message that's appropriate in the work-place. Your tendency to take this posture may be defensive, a subconscious effort to protect yourself from bad news or negative feedback.

Just as there is more to speaking than uttering a sequence of words, there is more to listening than processing the sounds that enter your ears. Sometimes the real message lies in what's *not* being said. It's important to listen between the lines to hear the unspoken messages. Pay attention to unspoken signals and nonverbal cues. When an employee says, "Yes, I'd be happy to research that informa-tion" in a high-pitched, tense voice, and she crosses her arms across her chest before she speaks, what is she really telling you? That she has enough work already without taking on more time-consuming assignments? That she's cold and wishes she'd brought her sweater to the meeting? That she can't stand the database librarian she'll have to contact to request the information? You can't know without asking further questions, but you should know there's more to the answer than the words she's spoken.

"The art of effective listening is essential to clear communication, and clear communication is necessary to management success."

—James Cash Penney, founder of J.C. Penney

Effective listening is an activity that requires your full and focused attention:

- Engage your mind to slow down your brain. Let it hear every word as if it were a delightful chocolate that you want to savor until it melts away, letting every molecule of flavor seep into your senses.
- Beware the familiarity trap. As soon as the words begin to sound familiar, the search for new information ends. "I've heard this before!" your mind says, and it turns its attention elsewhere. Bring it back! Most listening mistakes occur when you assume something that isn't so.
- Don't cross the line from anticipation to assumption. Anticipating someone's response or next question often helps you shape your end of the communication. But there's a fine line between

anticipating and assuming, and assuming will almost always get you in trouble.

- Maintain and keep eye contact, just as when you're speaking. This shows that you're listening and demonstrates your sincerity. It also helps you pick up on nonverbal cues.
- Don't formulate your response or mentally argue while the person is still speaking. You can't be listening to someone else if you're busy listening to yourself.

Nonverbal Language

Words are only a small percentage of the typical communication process—just 7 percent, in fact. Body language and nonverbal cues account for 55 percent, while 38 percent is the tone of voice. Dialogue that takes place over the telephone is missing over half the content of typical communication!

Listening effectively doesn't mean you have to let conversations roam where they will. You can, and often should, shape the direction of dialogue (at least in a business context). Use natural pauses to ask questions or make comments that keep the conversation on track. Learn when you can interrupt smoothly and effectively. Ask structured, open-ended questions to frame the subject yet allow the person to respond freely: "What happened when you opened the box and discovered that all the templates were reversed?"

EFFECTIVE TEAMWORK

Function As a Cohesive Unit

Some groups come together or "click" from the first time their members meet, while others labor for months or longer to be something other than separate and competing personalities. Creating an effective work group is part planning and part luck. Just as mixing chemicals produces different results depending on the substances and their quantities, combining personalities and work styles results in varied effects. Indeed, we often talk about the "chemistry" among group members as being critical to the group's success. Changing just one member often alters the group far beyond that one member's role and responsibilities.

EFFECTIVE TEAMWORK

A work group exists because a company hires a number of people to perform specific tasks and jobs. A team develops when those people work together in ways that enhance their efficiency and productivity. A team is a complex organism that exists as an entity in its own right and also as a collection of the individuals that comprise it. Individual personalities and work styles significantly influence the team's collective identity. The most effective teams contain complementary, not necessarily similar, personalities and work styles. In such a setting, the whole truly becomes more than the sum of its parts: a team. Each person's strengths overlap the others' weaknesses.

Sometimes teams form around job responsibilities. Certain people in marketing, like the PR group, are a natural team, as is the production control or quality control group in manufacturing. Teams also form that slice across responsibilities. For example, managers can pull together people from different jobs or departments to look at morale issues, evaluate new technologies, or help the department get ready to implement a new procedure or methodology. Such teams get people interacting in new ways by forming relationships that cut across the usual functional boundaries, especially when those boundaries also separate groups that compete with each other in some way. And when managers constantly bring different people together on various teams, employees learn to adapt better to change because they have to quickly become cohesive and then accomplish something.

Keep Things on an Even Keel

Generally, strong individual productivity generates strong group performance. When each member is pulling his or her load, the work gets done. Also, people feel that their contributions are both valued and valuable. Even with one or two weak members, most groups can maintain strong productivity. But the more pronounced the disparities in workload and contribution, the less satisfied all group members become—and then the group's performance suffers even though some individuals within the group are outstanding producers.

Teams develop not only a way of operating, but also of interacting. A culture forms that establishes the team's expectations and standards. Each team member has a role; this defines and distributes responsibility. In some teams, one person surfaces as the leader, often emerging naturally, although sometimes the manager designates the leader. In other teams, the members share leadership roles and responsibilities. While shared leadership is generally more effective in accomplishing the team's goals, much depends on the team itself—its goals and purpose as well as the personalities and work styles of its members.

WHERE DO YOU FIT IN?

As the work group's manager, shouldn't you be the team's leader? Well, yes and no. You are the leader in that you're the one with the authority to make decisions, and you will usually be the one held accountable for the group's actions, performance, and productivity. But in most situations, the manager isn't a team member. It's nearly impossible to be a team member and an authority figure concurrently. Teams function most effectively when there is a relatively even distribution of power so that each team member feels he or she is making an equitable contribution. As manager, it's your role to stay on the periphery. It's your job to be sure everyone knows his or her role and responsibilities, and the roles of other members. And you'll need to be available to serve as facilitator, mediator, teacher, mentor, cheerleader, coach, and parent—whatever the group needs.

Guiding the Team

When teams are working, there is nothing more exciting. But even teams that seem to come together well on their own need guidance and occasionally intervention to help them grow and develop. It's a balancing act that requires constant attention and adjustment. Just remember that this is about the team, not about you.

Acme Industries was a mega-corporation. Employees often joked that it was like its own little city; the corporate campus covered several square miles and included a daycare center, health clinic, fitness center, several cafeterias, and even a private security force that patrolled the grounds and facilities. There were many rules and restrictions—some company-wide, others specific to particular divisions, departments, or work groups.

Sheila was the education department's manager. Her department was both a microcosm of and a haven from the company's bureaucracy. Sheila had to enforce corporate rules and policies as well as keep the department on track with corporate goals and objectives. Daily policies such as leave time and working hours had to be consistent with the company's procedures.

Sheila recognized that it was important for people to feel that they had some control over their work and work environment. Although the corporation was enormous and complex, her department could succeed in meeting its goals only when its members could feel that they were more than just work units. Sheila encouraged both independence and teamwork among her employees, and gave them the latitude this balance required. Employees had to follow the company rules, but they could bend them on occasion to fit the needs of their assignments and projects. Team members could work off campus, for example, or order in lunch when work tasks became intense. The department was, in many ways, a haven from the rigid corporate culture.

Employees formed tight working relationships with one another. They had a high level of trust and a strong sense of belonging. They knew Sheila believed in their abilities to handle complex training projects as well as to resolve challenges that might arise within the group. And they knew Sheila was available to them when they needed her—to help with problem solving, to commiserate when stress levels escalated, to be a sounding board for new ideas. As a result, the department excelled in meeting its goals as well as helping the corporation to meet its goals. Absenteeism and turnover were extraordinarily low, and the department maintained a training schedule that would have swamped a less effective team. Sheila praised her department's efforts and contributions, both within the department and in her meetings and contacts with others in the company—her superiors as well as her peers. Her employees knew that she, and by extension the company, valued them.

Traits of an Effective Team

Effective teams share certain characteristics. First, they have a clear sense of mission or purpose, and they have clear goals. To be productive, team members need to know why they're working. When a work team knows its mission or purpose (reason for existing) and its goals (desired accomplishments), its members are more likely to focus on activities that move the group closer to completion—of tasks, of projects, of products or services.

Do They Have to Like Each Other to Be Effective?

As much as we'd like to think professionalism transcends petty matters like popularity, the reality is that people who like each other get along better. Certainly a team whose members provide complementary skills can function competently and even productively without friendship to bond them. But when team members consider themselves friends as well as colleagues, they have a heightened investment in the team's activities.

Second, effective teams foster mutual respect and support. It's hard to be innovative when you're never sure how others will react to your ideas. In effective teams, members know that even if coworkers disagree, they will focus their objections on the idea, not on the person presenting it. Each member feels he or she has the fundamental right to a level of trust that precludes backstabbing, gossip, and other negative behaviors. Members instead provide positive encouragement and work cooperatively to achieve common goals.

Effective teams demonstrate open communication. Team members are comfortable sharing ideas and concerns with each other as well as with you, their manager. Communication happens on numerous levels, from casual chitchat to structured meetings. While each level has its protocols and norms, openness is an essential foundation. Inherent in such communication is the ability to resolve disagreements, conflicts, and problems. No group (no matter how small, tight-knit, or productive) gets along all the time. The ability of team members to work through their differences to arrive at renewed levels of understanding and cooperation is crucial to the group's success. There will be squalls and occasionally storms, but conflict is a normal part of human interaction. The most effective groups have processes in place for airing grievances and working out problems.

Lastly, effective teams receive appropriate external support. Even the most self-sufficient, effective work teams can't function in a vacuum. They need you and your superiors (often viewed collectively as "the company"), and sometimes other departments or work groups, to provide the resources required to achieve their goals. Team members need the proper equipment and supplies, an appropriate workspace, adequate administrative support, and suitable environmental amenities (such as lighting and temperature control). It's your role as manager to be sure all of these elements are in place.

RESPONSIBILITY AND ACCOUNTABILITY

Keys to Your Success

As an employee, you were responsible for completing job tasks and work projects. You may have had limited authority to delegate certain responsibilities to others, but for the most part the line of authority ran in the other direction. Your manager delegated to you, and you carried out the assignment, though your manager bore the brunt of accountability for how well you did your work. When you succeeded, your manager got the bulk of the credit. When you failed, your manager took the fall.

Make a Fresh Start

When it becomes necessary to resolve a problem with an employee who reports to you, always offer the opportunity for a fresh start. The person should not feel compelled to continue a certain pattern of behavior with you. No matter the trail of angry words that follow the person into your office, stop them at the threshold. This lessens the pull of past behavior (however immediate that past is) and allows you to break off onto a new path that hopefully leads to resolution.

You're a manager yourself now. How you handle responsibility and accountability is often the single most important aspect of your position as manager and the key to your future success in management. Though you undoubtedly have a heavy load of responsibility, you have the authority to assign tasks and actions to the employees who report to you. You also accept accountability for their performance. We hope that when things go well you share the glory (along with any tangible rewards) with those who did the work. We also hope that when things turn out not so well, you have the fortitude to suck it up and take the hit. This is why you get paid the big bucks. Afterward, of course, there'll be time enough for constructive review of what went wrong. Accountability summarizes the concept of "the buck stops here."

The common perception is that accountability is related to negative consequences, the fallout from circumstances that go awry. But accountability also encompasses the positive consequences. When a project comes through and accomplishes its objectives, as its manager you are the first and most prominent to receive accolades. When things do go wrong, it's more effective and productive to look at the circumstance as an opportunity for learning—for employees and for you.

Lewis toiled long and hard as a computer programmer before his superiors finally took notice and promoted him to manager. The promotion was long overdue, Lewis felt, and he threw himself into his vision of a manager with great zeal. He felt important, he acted important, and most of the time, he rushed around looking important. Now that he had a real office, he closed the door whenever he was in it.

Not sure whether they should knock or just walk in, employees took to waiting for Lewis to emerge—which he did mostly when he needed something or to grandstand about his latest accomplishment (which always happened solely because of his extraordinary abilities, not because of any contributions from the department, to hear him tell it). When Lewis communicated at all with employees, it was through e-mail or Post-it notes left on their computer screens.

Lewis's behavior turned out to be self-sabotage. With no bond to him, people in the group short-circuited him. They failed to rally around projects. They fulfilled their responsibilities, but they did only what they had to do and nothing more. They made it clear to upper management and to Lewis's counterparts that they really had minimal interaction with Lewis. Ultimately upper management restructured department lines, which eliminated Lewis's department and job. While Lewis's employees all received transfers to other jobs within the company, Lewis got a severance package.

DAILY INTERACTIONS WITH YOUR EMPLOYEES

Making It Personal

It's amazing that many managers don't interact with their employees any more than they have to. This creates discomfort on both sides. Some of this stems from the way American businesses select managers: Those who excel in the skills of their jobs receive promotions to reward them for their abilities. The result is often managers who are not really people-people. They're skills-people. They're really great as accountants, programmers, sales representatives, or production workers who have done so well in their jobs that they've been promoted to management positions.

Don't Isolate Yourself

Employees need you to stop by every day and say hello. When you don't, they may assume something is wrong, or they may feel ignored. And when you don't interact with your employees, you begin to assume that they think and act in certain ways. From these assumptions, you draw conclusions that they are doing, or not doing, certain things. When we don't have information, we make it up. This is true for managers and employees alike.

As satisfying as these successful employees find it to be moving up the corporate food chain, they're still uncomfortable—sometimes with being in authority and often with the social expectations that come with the turf. Coming into management on the wave of ormance and productivity, many new managers get caught up in their own day-to-day responsibilities and don't see the bigger picture. They remain focused on doing a good job, failing to recognize that their role as a manager is to help everyone else do a good job, too. Bureaucracy, paperwork, and managing upwards (office politics) also take their toll, consuming more time and effort than managers and employees might feel is reasonable.

EFFECTIVE INFORMAL COMMUNICATION

Is small talk hard for you? That's okay. Communication is a craft each of us must learn. Although the ability to talk seems natural enough, circumstances that require structured dialogue can make otherwise competent adults sputter incoherently. So consider small talk just one of the new skills you must learn to excel at your job as a manager.

Each day, make it a point to stop by each employee's office, cubicle, desk, or work area. Greet the person with the name he or she uses when contacting you. If the employee's coworkers call him Mike, and his wife calls him Mitch, but he says, "This is Michael" when he calls you, then call him Michael. Or better yet, ask him what he prefers that you call him. Names often reflect a level of trust and equity; jumping to an informal variation (or using a formal variation when others don't) might make the person uncomfortable.

Ask each employee one question related to a personal interest. Yes, this might require you to do a little research. Careful listening can help you to build a mental "information file" about each employee. The general question, "How was your weekend?" can elicit an astonishing breadth and depth of information. Ask each employee one work-related question. If this is new behavior for you, employees might react with suspicion at first, thinking you're checking up on them (which you are, in a sense) or that something is wrong (which probably isn't the case).

The Right Title

In most job settings today, people within one or two corporate levels of each other use first names when talking with or about each other. In some situations, protocol requires using professional or courtesy titles: Dr. Drake, Mr. Johnson, Ms. Hernandez, Sgt. Hamilton, Officer Michaels, and so forth. Sometimes employees use these titles only in public or when customers are present; in other settings, they use them all the time.

As employees realize these interactions are now part of your daily routine, they'll warm up. The first sign of progress is when they start telling you about things that are going wrong. But you know you're in your groove when they start telling you about things that are going right.

COMMUNICATION THROUGH WRITING

No discussion of communication is complete without mentioning the importance of effective writing skills. No matter what their position or level in the company, at some point all employees must put words on paper. You might need to write a memo, a report, or a performance appraisal. What you say matters; how you say it can matter more. Although writing is a life skill, not just a job skill, many people turn into babbling bureaucrats when they write. There's no reason for business writing to be any more convoluted than talking. In fact, it can be easier to write because you focus just on your presentation. In fact, it's as easy as three steps that you can view as your AIM:

- **A**udience: Who will read your message?
- **I**ntent: Why are you writing?
- **M**essage: What do you have to say?

Make separate lists to answer each of these three questions. Then use your lists as an outline and begin writing. Write as though your audience is sitting in front of you and you are talking to them. Hold the slang, but stay conversational. Write enough content (your message) to cover your intent—no more. Be sure the vocabulary you choose is appropriate for your audience; steer clear of jargon.

Keep It Simple

Consider this advice from *The Elements of Style*, a staple on writers' bookshelves: "A sentence should contain no unnecessary words, a paragraph no unnecessary sentences. . . . This requires not that the writer make all his sentences short, or that he avoid all detail and treat his subjects only in outline, but that every word tell."

Don't let the process of writing intimidate you. It's just another form of communication. The best way to begin writing is to start with what's on your mind. Keep in mind that you don't have to start at the beginning. You can rearrange your blocks of words after you get them down on paper (or on screen). Word processing programs and computers make this very easy. Often one idea flows into the next once you get started, leading you through all of what you want to say. And remember, nobody gets it just right the first time. Writing is a process of editing and revising. If you don't like the way something sounds, change it.

KEEP IT CONCISE

To keep your focus clear and clean, make sure every sentence contributes to your intent and message in a way that is relevant to your audience. The myriad details of last month's focus group might fascinate you, but the employees receiving your report just need to know the problems and the suggestions for remedying them. The typical manager gives a written document, paper or electronic, about eight seconds to prove itself worthy of further interest and more time. Brevity counts!

E-MAIL ISSUES

Ironically, it's the proliferation of electronic communication that most graphically illustrates the need to address writing skills. The speed with which we can zip messages across the office or around the world makes us behave as though we must take every available shortcut to save even more time, circumventing the processes that effective writing requires. The instantaneous nature of e-mail makes us feel as though we have to read and write at the same speed. But we don't (and can't), and trying to do this is often a direct route to misunderstanding. The same guidelines for effective communication on paper apply in the paperless environment of the Internet.

Because e-mail is instantaneous, it's easy to fire off responses and comments without thinking about potential ramifications. The fact that most of us delete e-mail messages once we've read or sent them gives us the impression that they are temporal communications, existing only in time just like conversations in person or over the phone (and just as private). Wrong! This is a common and potentially hazardous belief. A growing number of companies capture and store electronic messages that travel through the company's networked computer systems. So far the courts have upheld the rights of companies to do this; what you do on company time with company resources belongs to the company and is the company's business.

If you wouldn't write something in a printed letter or a memo, then don't write it in an e-mail message, either. With distribution lists and bulk forwarding, the message you send to your superior "for your eyes only" could end up on hundreds of other computers. E-mail messages have embarrassed presidents and secretaries alike, and they are an increasing source of evidence in legal proceedings involving everything from sexual harassment to wrongful termination. That offhand comment you fire off in response to a question about someone's performance could become an electronic ghost that returns to haunt you months or years from now.

The Importance of Detail

Another problem with e-mail is that it's so easy we tend to forget some essential steps that seem much more natural when we have to write something out by hand. Be sure to take the following steps with any e-mail you send:

- Proofread it before you hit Send. Look for misspelled words, missing words, or awkward grammatical constructions. Such things, if left in, mark you as being sloppy and indicate that you lack attention to detail.

- Read the e-mail over slowly, making sure it says what you need it to say. If possible, close the door to your office and read it out loud.

- Write the text of the e-mail first. Then, when you've read it through and proofed it, fill in the subject line and, last of all, the name of the person to whom it's going. That avoids the possibility of hitting Send before you're ready to do so.

WHAT WORKS FOR THEM WORKS FOR YOU

Continuous Learning

As a manager, working hard to support your employees with job training and skill improvement activities can make you feel really good. Go ahead and take a minute or so to enjoy the good feeling. Then take a few steps back and look at the bigger picture. Unless you're a working manager with job responsibilities that are similar to those of the employees you manage, it's probably not necessary for your skills to match those of your employees. Still, you need to know enough about their jobs to determine whether your employees need additional training and if so, in what. Subscribe to newsletters and magazines that are relevant for your industry or field. Ask employees what publications they would find useful. Web-based resources are abundant, too, and are becoming increasingly sophisticated.

Advanced Degrees

Many companies require managers to have at least a bachelor's degree. Though experience within the industry is also crucial, the market for managers has become so competitive that education level is often a screening criterion for job candidates. Obtaining appropriate advanced degrees or certifications could help you rise through the ranks of management. In many cases, companies will give managers financial assistance to go to school in pursuit of advanced degrees that are relevant to their job.

Does your company have an education support program that provides tuition reimbursement and other benefits for employees who go back to school? Many colleges offer evening classes and distance learning programs by computer, targeting working adults who want to advance their formal education. Many companies have education requirements, such as a graduate degree, for managers. This is most likely the case if you work in an industry where the people who report to you have advanced degrees or high levels of education. Even entry-level positions that are on the company's promotion track are likely to have minimum education requirements that may not have applied to you before you joined the management team. If your education is in a specialty field, you may desire further education in another field or in a broader area.

Progressive companies support ongoing education and training for employees at all levels. Larger companies may have their own programs to teach management skills, or they might be willing to send new managers to outside programs. Commit to updating and expanding your skills and expertise, and encourage your employees to do the same. You can never know too much!

GROWING GOOD PEOPLE

Training and Improving Your Team

Once, perhaps back when you first entered the workforce, it was enough to land a job. It wasn't so long ago that working people were happy to simply receive paychecks, and employers were glad to have productive employees. But times have changed. Today, both employers and employees recognize that there's a difference between a job and a career. People no longer stay in the same job or work for the same company for all of their working lives. On average, people have up to seven different careers and work for a dozen or more companies from the time they enter the workforce until the time they leave it. More of either is not uncommon.

Their Own Goals

Encourage employees to come up with two or three personal goals. An employee might set a goal to complete a specialty training program, undergraduate degree, or graduate degree. This accomplishment would clearly benefit the employee, but it has benefits for the company as well by making the employee more promotable or, at the very least, more knowledgeable.

Your company entrusts you with its most valuable resource—employees. It expects you to help your employees develop their skills and careers. Sometimes you want to do this anyway because your employees are good people who work hard and you want to see them grow. You don't want to lose them, and you know they might quit without appropriate support. Sometimes you need employees to grow so that they can take on more responsibilities—and free you up for the same reason. If employees don't feel like they are growing, they become stagnant. Over time, the department too will become stagnant and so will the organization. It often doesn't require that much for you to provide the learning opportunities that your employees want and need. You might try the following:

- Create a departmental training committee so that employees can assess training needs and present ideas for meeting them
- Ask employees with particular proficiency in certain areas to conduct short workshops for other employees
- Sponsor brown-bag lunch training sessions in which experts from other parts of the company or outside sources conduct short presentations during lunch breaks
- Establish a mentoring program in which employees pair up to learn from each other

Use regular feedback to help employees improve their skills and performance. Suggest different approaches to achieve better outcomes. Make sure that feedback is relevant to the employee. Focus on how he or she approaches job tasks and work responsibilities. Take care not to compare or criticize the employee's work style if it differs from yours.

Conflict Resolution

With the shift in today's business environment from a domineering management approach to one that is more collaborative, managers often benefit from training in conflict resolution and mediation techniques.

It might be your preference to work on an assignment without having your superiors checking in with you all the time and telling you what a good job you're doing. And that's fine—it works for you. It is easy to assume all people work the same way or should be the same way, particularly if you have some employees who are like you in terms of work style. Being among people who share your characteristics reinforces your attitudes and behaviors.

A key element of retaining the best people is to give constant feedback. In fact, some employees will request this and will function less well if they don't get it. Your perspective and work style might set you up to think that employees who need a lot of feedback are just brown-nosing to stay in good with the boss. Although of course office politics come into play with all people (even you) at times, there's a strong likelihood that these employees are just people who need the sense of structure that constant feedback provides. For such people, the manager is the one who defines the work group and its functions and thus is the most logical choice to go to for feedback. After all, you set the standards, and ultimately it's you who must be satisfied with the results.

This is reality—for you and for your employees. Make sure they each have the same opportunities to showcase their successes and achievements for you and they'll be more likely to stay with the company. Just be sure you know whether that apple-polishing employee is advancing the goals of the team and the company or is just feeding the beast. Take the time to ferret out the true objective before you come to a conclusion. When an employee attempts to communicate with you at the expense of the team leader or coworkers, send the employee back to the group to communicate appropriately. Sometimes the employees doing the most communicating have the most time to do so because the real performers are too busy doing the work.

MANAGING DISTANCED EMPLOYEES

Working with Telecommuters

As of 2016, it was estimated that at least 60 million people in the United States worked away from their offices at least some of the time. This number has grown since, and there's every reason to think it will continue to do so. The improvement of communication technology makes telecommuting a viable option for almost everyone.

With this growth has come increased challenges for managers of remote employees. It's all too easy for these employees to become mentally separated from their work, and a manager must work hard to keep these physically distant employees engaged.

WHAT MAKES A GOOD TELECOMMUTER?

If a member of your team asks to work from out of the office, full time or part time, you should consider some questions about her or him.

- Is the person results-oriented, with excellent communication skills?
- Does she have a solid knowledge of her job with a good understanding of corporate goals and objectives?
- Is she organized, with good time-management skills?

If the answers to these questions are yes, go on to consider the job itself as well as the atmosphere in which the employee will be working. Are the job tasks clearly defined, with definite goals? Is the work well suited to telework? Is the employee's home (or wherever she'll be working from) conducive to productive telework? Does your company have the IT infrastructure to support her?

Geographically Dispersed Teams

These days it's not unusual for some team members—possibly including some management teams—to be separated from one another by many miles, or even continents. Such groups are referred to as geographically dispersed teams (GDTs). While managing them can present many challenges, such an arrangement allows upper management more flexibility in hiring the right people.

All these (and probably other) questions go to the heart of successful telecommuting: Will the employee be as successful and productive while working from home as she is from the office?

Setting Up a Home Office

If your team member is going to work from home on a regular basis, he'll need a well-equipped office from which to do it. In discussing the matter with him, make sure that his office includes the following:

- A computer with Internet access and e-mail
- A printer/scanner
- A phone with voicemail; it's better if this phone is separate from the employee's personal line
- A desk and comfortable chair in a quiet area of the house, free of distractions

It may be necessary for you to actually travel to the employee's home and inspect the facilities he'll be using.

AVOID ISOLATION

One of the biggest issues that you must deal with in managing remote employees is preventing them from feeling isolated, cut off from the rest of the company. This can be a bigger problem for those workers who telecommute all the time rather than just a few days a week.

Steps you can take to prevent this include:

1. Have regular team meetings in which the telecommuting employee participates
2. Schedule times when the telecommuter comes into the office to get face time with her fellow workers, as well as face-to-face meetings with you and other managers
3. Have weekly phone calls with the employee
4. If company-wide meetings are held, arrange for the employee to listen live. If this isn't possible, send a recording of the meeting to the employee

E-mail

E-mail is among your most important tools in successfully managing telecommuters. It gives you instant communication, keeping the employee up to date with everything that's going on in the company. At the same time, you must be careful not to suggest in any way that your expectations of the employee's performance are different from those you have of workers who show up to the office every day.

Videoconferencing

Videoconferences are an excellent way to involve remote employees in the day-to-day work of the team. Most computers these days have some capacity for this; it's also possible to do this using Skype. The important thing is that everyone should be able to see one another, which helps psychologically to reduce the distance between team members.

Overall, it's essential that you, as manager, make remote team members feel just as valued and included as everyone else.

DOES MONEY MATTER?

The Importance of Salary

Especially in times of economic upturn when there are more opportunities to switch jobs, employees look for positive reasons to stay with a company. One of the most important of these reasons is salary, whick makes it easier for workers to meet their material needs.

MONEY MATTERS

The harsh reality in the business world is that companies have to make a profit. Businesses must balance profitability, customer or client satisfaction, and quality products or services. (Even not-for-profit organizations must meet their financial goals and keep their constituents happy.) While high-level money matters can create tensions in the office, remember one thing: Your employees care about profit, too. Though they try to choose jobs they enjoy, most people work because they need to earn an income.

Dissatisfiers versus Satisfiers

Sometimes money talks and employees walk—to competitors who offer deals that are too good to refuse. But for the most part, money moves up and down on an employee's list of dissatisfiers (things he or she does not like about the job) rather than on the list of satisfiers (things he or she likes about the job).

It used to be that there was a set salary range for a position, and it established the boundaries for negotiation. It was a range that didn't vary much from company to company for positions at the same relative level of management. Most people started at the lower end of the scale, ostensibly so there would be incentive for them to improve (which really meant giving them raises for staying in the job). Those with exceptional abilities or unique skills might have started at the middle of the range. Few started at the top; those who had the qualifications to do so were probably overqualified for the job in the first place, so the reasoning went, and would soon move on when it became clear that there was no room for advancement within the position. Money and ability were like twins, seldom separated. Like bell-bottoms and tie-dye shirts, this is a vestige of a bygone era. Today, salaries are often open territory.

Salary versus Benefits

According to the U.S. Bureau of Labor Statistics, an employee's salary represents about three-fourths of the company's direct compensation costs for having the employee on staff. Benefits (such as insurance, paid time off, and retirement plans) account for the remainder.

In today's marketplace, salary is subject to a number of factors. Some companies that have seen extraordinary success pay their employees substantially above the market average. In other cases, salary levels depend on the local cost of living. In still other instances, a comparatively low salary may be balanced against higher-than-normal benefits.

In discussing salary with your employees, be sure to have the full facts in hand before the conversation. This includes information on what comparable companies in the area are paying workers doing similar jobs; a clear notion of the value of the benefits the company offers; and possible options for either a salary increase (within the company's mandated range) or an idea of something else you can offer.

Never ask for details of an employee's financial circumstances. If she or he wants to tell you, that's fine, but it's a sensitive subject, and you shouldn't pry. If a worker wants more money, let him or her explain why.

CHANNELING CREATIVE ENERGY

Promoting Innovation

Creativity is a more abstract area of job satisfaction than money. Nonetheless, it's equally—if not more—important to employees. Nearly every job involves some aspect of creativity, from jobs we consider to be creative (such as media or teaching) to those we think of as being more mundane (such as accounting or cleaning). Creativity covers the spectrum of innovation, from the ability to see new ways to accomplish familiar tasks to the capacity to envision entirely new processes or products.

The Productivity Sweet Spot

Some people require constant direction, feedback, and redirection. Others are better left to a general framework within which they are free to structure the job's tasks, flow, and progress measures. Consider how each employee works most productively, and then shape your oversight and interactions such that they are appropriate within the context of the employee's work style.

Creativity and productivity are not mutually exclusive, although channeling creativity into productivity can be a significant challenge for a manager. You just need to identify people who are naturally creative thinkers and make sure they have the flexibility—in terms of assignments and environment—to express their creativity. How can you stimulate and support productive creativity without squelching the creative process? You might try these ideas:

- Present assignments in general terms, explaining the desired end result but allowing employees the latitude to find their own ways to that result. Establish timelines to keep productivity on track, but don't structure the work process.
- Allow people to express risky ideas without immediately shooting them down. "Let me play devil's advocate" is the surest way to cut creative thinking off at the knees.
- Let people work through mistakes to find their own solutions, and allow time for this as part of the creative process. It takes a lot of coal to make diamonds.
- Learn how to praise someone's efforts without focusing on the result or product you want those efforts to generate.
- Ask employees what you can do to provide a stimulating and supportive environment. You might be surprised at how simple some of their requests will be.
- Sponsor workshops that are conducted by outside resources. Creative people are always looking to broaden their base of knowledge and expertise. New faces bring fresh perspectives. Employees are sometimes more willing to question and raise issues with outsiders than they are with internal trainers or consultants.

Remember, though, that new approaches are sometimes threatening. Employees and managers feel like their necks are on the line these days, and no one likes to take risks that will stretch theirs. Because many people, up and down the corporate ladder, notice changes, many managers take the easy route and stay with the tried and true, no matter how tired or even nonproductive that approach has become. This reflects an insecurity that employees pick up on, even if you yourself don't. But it's critical for managers and employees to take risks now and again, to explore new ways of doing things.

Familiarity breeds repetition, which soon becomes complacency and stagnation. No company, no matter what its products or services, can thrive (or even survive) without fresh ideas.

Creative Jobs

Although you can find them in just about any job, creative people tend to gravitate toward creative jobs—work that requires them to come up with new processes or products. These jobs are often in fields such as advertising, marketing, electronic media, publishing, design, and architecture. You might define these people as writers, artists, or programmers, or they might have a combination of talents that defies definition.

Creative people tend to make managers a little nervous—it's hard to tell sometimes whether they're working or goofing off, and they seem a bit, well, unleashed. Creative types can often be characterized as follows:

- They appear to have little regard for authority, rules, structure, and routine, viewing these as elements of the work world that do not apply to them.
- They establish surroundings within their work environments that support and feed their imaginations.
- They have unorthodox or eccentric methods for stimulating their productivity.
- They appear disorganized and seem to "fly by the seat of their pants" when giving presentations.
- They find humor in, and even make fun of, just about everything (and might not understand why others may find these "funnies" either unfunny or offensive).
- They work in spurts of intensity that can last for hours, days, or even weeks, and then go into a "down" phase, when they appear to accomplish very little.

- They arrive late or even fail to show up for staff or other general meetings that don't apply directly to their projects.

People in creative professions may require tremendous flexibility in terms of management. Emotion, not logic, rules their creative process. The result is often behavior that goes beyond what others might consider conventional business behavior. The office of a creative person might look more like a preschool classroom or a toy store than a workstation. Creative types also need to be able to shut themselves away, to get away from the structure of rules and decorum, so as to give their ideas space and time to evolve.

Companies or departments that rely on creative people, such as advertising agencies or media companies, often use brainstorming sessions to accomplish work objectives. To the uninitiated (or those who require structure) these sessions might appear to be wild free-for-alls. People laugh, yell, throw things, draw pictures, and tell jokes as they toss about ideas. Political correctness stays in the hall; there's plenty of opportunity later to run the censor filters. The entire mission is to let brains wander freely through the vast seed bins of ideas until some start to sprout.

Appearances Are Deceiving

Despite appearances to the contrary, most creative people are highly organized. It's just that the organization doesn't necessarily take the form of neatly labeled files and calendars that record meetings and commitments—the standard trappings of structure. Those "seat of the pants" presentations often reflect not lack of preparation but instead a deeply assimilated knowledge of the topic acquired through intense and often extended research or observation—sometimes with a dash of intuition thrown in. This less tangible style of organization can have the appearance of chaos, but it's not. For the creative individual, it's as close to logical as it gets.

Building a Creative Atmosphere

Many companies in creative businesses have lounge areas with pool tables, coffee bars, video games, bean bag chairs, and other diversions to get people relaxed and thinking. Such an atmosphere creates an oasis from the reality of business (which is of course why the creative professionals are employed in the first place). Once ideas take on viable shapes, creative types retreat into the cocoons of their offices. They re-emerge when they've created something from those shapes that they're ready to share with others or that now needs feedback.

Not surprisingly, too much structure stifles creativity. As a manager, this can be a difficult balancing act for you. On the one hand you have a creative genius (or even a team of creative geniuses) whose ideas generate most of the products that make your company successful. On the other hand, you have the company that wants to make sure the time it pays for is productive. Perhaps you are also responsible for managing other people whose work is more traditional and who might believe that anyone who's having so much fun at work isn't working hard enough.

RECOGNIZING AND NURTURING POTENTIAL

The Inner Light

Cultivate the talents and abilities of people who already work for your company whenever possible. Your company already has a considerable investment in its employees, and statistics show that employees promoted from within are more likely to succeed as managers than are new hires brought into management positions.

As a manager, you have the obligation to help employees identify their potential (that is, you have to put on your coach or your mentor hat). The first step is to ask the employee what he or she wants to achieve, and what route appears likely to travel in that direction. What obstacles exist? How can the employee overcome them? Are the employee's perceptions of ability and potential the same as yours? If not, why?

Opportunity is a significant element of equity an employee builds in her or his job. For an employee, career satisfaction means opportunity for growth as well as recognition. As a manager your task is to assess how this person can best contribute, now and in the future, as an individual. Opportunities come alive for people when you, as a manager, take the time and interest to assess their interests and work with them to help realize their potential. Such opportunities are not always obvious or what they seem. To help cultivate an employee's potential, you could do the following:

- Send the employee to several work-related seminars and conferences each year.

- Invite the employee to accompany you to a meeting or event that he or she otherwise wouldn't be able to attend.
- Incorporate a discussion of future goals and objectives into every formal performance evaluation, including follow-ups from previous evaluations.
- Ask each employee several times a year what you can do to support his or her career aspirations. Pay attention to goals that change; goals *should* change if the employee is making any progress toward meeting them.

Ongoing training or continuing education is often required for many technical and professional staff, though such education could be easy to overlook when it comes to support staff. While a course in computer code might hold little appeal for an administrative assistant, a class in creating PowerPoint presentations might. Every now and then, if your budget allows, let employees attend workshops that aren't directly related to their jobs but that interest them for some reason. A technician might enjoy a class in graphic design, or a sales representative might like to go to a seminar on construction methods. Some choices might seem a bit far afield, but most people will choose options that appeal to their longer-term goals.

Say "Thank You"

Take time to thank the person in the mailroom, your secretary, or the department coordinator. It's easy to praise the people who do the most obvious tasks, but don't forget about all the others who work to make those tasks possible.

THE RISKS OF PLAYING FAVORITES

A Danger to Avoid

Favoritism is generally a personal matter. A manager likes someone, so he or she gives that person breaks. Sometimes favoritism is obvious; other times it's subtle. In every case, however, favoritism divides. It pits employees against each other (not always consciously), forcing them to compete for your attention. No one likes to feel left out or passed over. Experiencing these feelings as adults often recalls memories of unpleasant situations from childhood. It's one thing to compete for something and lose because the winner is truly better. It's quite another to lose because you didn't have a chance in the first place. Sometimes favoritism arises from a genuine desire to do something good for an employee that then evolves into a mentor-turned-monster scenario. Often favoritism exists as a form of office politics, with employees jockeying for position in the kiss-my-shoes line.

A Favoritism Example

Beware! Favoritism can come back to bite you before you know what happened. Here's an example.

Phillip came to work one day and dropped a bombshell on his manager's desk: his letter of resignation. He'd had it, he said; what had once been a very pleasant work environment was now a nightmare. He was tired of the complaining and the backstabbing and the lack of cooperation from certain others in the office. And now he'd been passed over for a project he'd proposed in last month's staff meeting. The project went instead to one of those others.

"Those others" were a small clique everyone called "Jean's disciples." They had coffee every morning with Jean, the department manager. Throughout the day, Jean called on one or more of these employees to run errands and handle special assignments. Because the work team continued to produce results, Jean was oblivious to the dynamics of the workplace. Other team members could see that she was out of touch, but Jean didn't respond to their hints. By the time Jean realized there was trouble, she was holding a valued employee's resignation letter.

In many ways, Jean was lucky the only cost to her and to the company was the loss of Phillip's employment. Though that cost continued because Phillip took a position with a competitor, things could've been much worse. Often, circumstances of favoritism end up as harassment claims, when the favoritism fades, or as discrimination claims from employees who are denied opportunities.

Star Players

When an employee truly does bring a special and highly valued talent or ability to your department, of course you must recognize that in some way. High performers need constant challenges to keep them interested and motivated. They need new responsibilities, recognition and praise, and higher salaries. At the same time, it's important—and essential—for you to make it clear that you are committed to providing opportunities for all employees who report to you. As valuable as one person might be, your department cannot succeed in meeting its goals without the full cooperation and collaboration of all its members.

Nowhere is this delicate balancing act more obvious than in professional sports. The news media overflow with stories about the astronomical salaries of talented young stars, many of whom have little experience going into the professional arena but who appear to have potential the team simply can't live without. Talent, of course, isn't everything. Yet talent leads many young athletes, even unproven in the professional arena, to believe they are entitled to such riches and rewards. In sports that have salary caps limiting the amount of money a team can spend overall for players, such high-cost players can prevent the team from keeping or acquiring other valuable players.

"Practice Golden-Rule 1 of Management in everything you do. Manage others the way you would like to be managed."

—Brian Tracy, business consultant

The business world is no different. When "star players" come into the company at inflated salaries or with other benefits that other employees don't get, it's difficult to maintain any sense of fairness. And when entire companies build around such inflation, it doesn't take a crystal ball to see that eventually the balloon will pop.

REALISTIC GOALS

Getting Everyone on the Same Page

How do you determine whether someone is putting an appropriate level of thought or creativity into the job? And with people working in teams, how do you figure out what each person should be doing? Every job has specific, core tasks as well as general responsibilities. Most jobs require interactions among employees to generate the products or services that are the company's reason for existing. Though the job description specifies such functions, it is your role as manager to establish the criteria for completing them. Such criteria vary widely among jobs but often include project timelines, production schedules, and unit of completion goals.

Dividing Into Groups

In some companies, it might be useful to divide the department or team into groups, each of which tackles a specific company goal, department goal, or job responsibility. If the process represents a major overhaul, consider starting with a task force that comes up with the initial take on what the standards should be.

Managers often have high expectations for their employees, and they become frustrated, disappointed, and angry when employees fail to live up to those expectations. That happens because these expectations are as much about the manager as they are about the employee. When your employees excel, you look good, too. Employees also often feel grateful to their managers for providing opportunities and encouragement. All of this strokes the manager's ego. When employees fail to meet expectations, managers feel hurt and let down.

Sometimes you might identify too closely with an employee. Perhaps the employee reminds you of yourself in an earlier stage of your career or is at risk of going down a path that you believe will be a mistake. You want this person to do well or even better than you have done. So you invest in this person—you provide opportunities, recognition, support, and encouragement. You may have high expectations for comparable investments in return, such as the willingness to arrive early and stay late to meet deadlines or accommodate a heavy workload. Such expectations are often unrealistic and become distortions. You might interpret an employee's unwillingness to work day and night as an attack on your values and authority rather than seeing it for what it is—an infringement on the employee's life beyond work.

It's not always easy to see that you're doing this, and it may be even harder to stop when you make the recognition. Ask yourself: Is this about them or me? Be honest. It's not always a bad thing for your expectations to be about you even when they involve others, but it is essential for you to know when this is the case.

Establish boundaries, within the framework of specific job requirements, around your expectations. Performance evaluation standards and job descriptions, as much as they may feel intrusive and bureaucratic, can help save you from yourself. When problems do arise, take two steps back to identify them clearly. Are you angry because the employee failed to complete an assignment, and now others can't complete theirs? Or are you upset because you can't showcase the project at this afternoon's staff meeting as you had planned? Put your effort into addressing the real problem.

GETTING SKIN IN THE GAME

People are most likely to accept and comply with performance standards if they have a role in establishing them. In many companies and industries, certain standards are carved in stone—set by regulation or outside authority, or are inherent in the work. Hospitals, colleges, universities, and other kinds of organizations are subject to quality expectations established by accrediting bodies. Failing to meet these standards means they cannot remain in business. Standards that apply to the organization trickle down through all levels and become imbedded in job descriptions as well as performance evaluation procedures. Within these standards, there may or may not be room for variation, depending on the industry.

Make It Work!

Whatever system your department or company uses to set performance standards, as manager it's your job to make it work. If employees suspect that their participation has been an exercise in futility, it's all over for collaboration and teamwork. This is an invitation to frustration, disappointment, and office politics.

Even when it appears that there is little latitude for employee participation for setting standards, there are usually small areas open to influence. For example, a hospital must require employees in patient-care areas to wear certain clothing and protective aids to safeguard them against exposure to infectious diseases. Allowing employees to choose clothing in various colors, patterns, and designs gives them a dress code they can live with because they developed it.

Implementation and Adjustment

There's more to meeting performance standards than personal satisfaction. Salaries, as well as any bonuses, generally depend on how well employees meet the performance standards. Some companies assign a percentage value to each standard. While sending follow-up notes might be worth just 2 percent, this function is essential to client satisfaction which, in turn, might be worth 25 percent of the total points. This kind of a system gives weighted importance to key functions, yet makes all activities essential to the whole.

Support Individual Growth

Employees are not at their jobs simply because they have nothing to do all day or because they want to save the world. They want to grow or at least to make more money. And they want you, their manager, to show them how they can do this. Any performance evaluation process should include short- and long-term personal goals. These goals, perhaps more so than department and company goals, change and evolve. For each employee, consider the following questions:

- What steps does the employee need to take to grow in the job and the department?
- What reward can the employee expect for achieving such growth?
- Where can the employee expect to go next in his or her career?
- What are the employee's prospects a few years down the road?

Of course, it's essential to have the employee participate in formulating personal goals, since manager and employee will need to agree to these goals. It's also important for you to help employees identify their strengths, where those strengths can take them, and how they might change or improve their options by taking certain training courses or learning special skills. (Are you wearing your mentor hat?) If you can't help an employee honestly define his or her next career goal, you're showing the employee a brick wall.

The Importance of Performance Standards

Performance standards, while somewhat bureaucratic, are also a way of ensuring both the perception and practice of fair treatment—which is something managers and employees alike desire.

With employees whose abilities shine, this is an easy as well as enjoyable part of your job. It's exciting to watch people grow and develop and reach their potential. But some people choose career objectives that their skills and abilities don't support. As a mentor, you can help such employees find paths that are better aligned with their talents—or find ways for them to successfully pursue the directions that interest them.

MAKE YOUR DAY PRODUCTIVE

Streamline Your Tasks

Most people have at least some difficulty in managing their time. When difficulties arise, we sometimes start apportioning blame:

- "They moved the goal posts on me again!"
- "He always wants everything yesterday."
- "If only I wasn't interrupted every five minutes, I could actually do some work."
- "I've spent the whole day answering the phone."

We all do it, but have you noticed how simple it is to blame everyone or everything else for difficulty in handling your time?

"So are you saying that it is all my own fault, then?" you might ask. Of course not! Our job and the people we work with make demands on our time, but "blame" isn't the issue here. Assigning blame might make us feel better, but doesn't solve the problem.

The solution to effective time management lies in your *attitude*. People who admit they have difficulty with time management will be 90 percent closer to solving the problem when they take responsibility for their own actions. There are only so many hours a day, and it's up to you how to spend them—either doing the work that's supposed to be done or letting interruptions and other distractions take time away from what you need to do. No improvement is likely, however, unless you recognize that the only person who can positively change anything on this score is *you*.

It is very difficult to change the habits and practices of others. So ask yourself what you do (or don't do) that contributes to the problem. And how you, personally, can change the situation. Write down some possible solutions. You'll likely find you have more control than you initially thought, and you can at least do something to help remedy the problem.

URGENT IS NOT NECESSARILY IMPORTANT

It's amazing how easily we confuse "urgent" with "important."

For example, what happens when the phone rings? Ninety-nine percent of the time, you pick it up. Telephones seem to have a way of instilling a feeling of urgency; by the very act of their ringing, they demand to be answered.

But the telephone itself isn't the problem. Rather, it's the issue being conveyed by the caller, often some "urgent" but minor problem. Just because something is "urgent" does not always mean that it is important. Yet because of their very immediacy, and the fact that they often center on deadlines, urgent items always seem to gain priority.

So how do we separate the wheat from the chaff so to speak, the urgent from the important? First, simply try not to react to pressure over an urgent item. Add it to your to-do list and prioritize it (high, medium, or low), based on both "urgency" and "importance." Deal with other items in the same way, remembering that:

- High urgency is the need for something to be done immediately.
- High importance is that which relates to a crucial objective—that is, something with a real impact.

Then look at your to-do list and decide in what order the various tasks should be done. Tasks high in both urgency and importance are done immediately, with the necessary time spent on them. Items that are urgent but unimportant should be done quickly, but you should not spend much time on them. It might help to set a time limit for each item.

Also note tasks that are important but not urgent—training and maintenance activities, for instance. Make sure to schedule these tasks so they are not "moved to the side" by urgent and/or unimportant tasks.

WRITE IT DOWN— AND MAKE IT REAL

"To do" lists would be a wonderful invention if only they didn't seem to grow faster than we can reduce them. Some people believe "to do" lists ought to be written on a roll of toilet paper because they just get longer and longer. Not only is this a practical thought but a recyclable one!

Most people keep some sort of list of things to do—in a book, on Post-it notes, and so forth. Not only can these become cumbersome, they can also be lost. "I had a little note about that here somewhere," they might say while searching frantically through mounds of paper.

There are a couple of ways to handle a to-do list. The first would be to put down tasks in a diary, either electronic or paper. The list would then be in the same place as your appointments and meetings. This approach has two advantages:

1. The list is less likely to be mislaid—unless you lose your diary!
2. By assigning the tasks to particular days, they are more visible—most people usually look at a diary at least daily. Therefore, you're more likely to accomplish the tasks when they should be done rather than leaving them to the last minute.

"But what if I don't do, or finish, something?" you might ask. Write it into the next available day. Duplication irritates, so there is a built-in motivation to get it done instead of rewriting it over and over again.

A second way to handle a to-do list is to purchase a wipe-off white board and place it prominently in your workspace. If you see it daily, you can keep track of various projects. There is also a sense of satisfaction when you wipe out a task (though of course it will be replaced with a new one).

Regardless of what system you use, the act of crossing off a completed task provides a feeling of accomplishment even as it reminds you what there is left to do that day. An added benefit of recording all of the tasks is that it reduces any worry that you will forget to do something. Although you may never complete all of the tasks, it will not be because you forgot but because you chose to complete another activity.

Any System Is Fine As Long As It Is Yours

Let's face it, there's a lot of pressure to purchase the latest "bell and whistle" that will supposedly help us master time, whether it's an electronic system, an all-in-one cell phone, or an expensive leather planner. Shell out a few hundred dollars, and voilà—your time-management problems will be solved!

If only ... All too often these systems force you into doing things their way, which may not help you achieve what you want. Or the system may be so complicated that you waste time figuring out how to plan your day. Regardless, as a consequence only a small part of the system is actually used if it's used at all.

In truth, any system will work, as long as it's compatible with your work habits. If writing a to-do list on the back of an envelope works, then do that. Likewise, if using a very expensive leather-bound system makes you feel good and spurs you to manage your time more effectively, that's fine too. Bottom line: Your system must suit you and your work habits and style.

If your present system leaves something to be desired, jot down what any new system must do for you. Then, and only then, should you look at the available options. Be sure to include those options that modify your existing system.

If you do use a computerized time management system make sure it can sync with your calendar. That way all records will be consistent and you'll avoid writing everything down twice (which in itself can lead to errors).

DON'T RUSH AROUND AIMLESSLY— ORGANIZE A ROUTINE DAY

Have you noticed how some people appear to be more organized than others? They react immediately to every call on their time—the latest demand is always the one they tackle right now. However, what they should be doing is often different from what they actually are accomplishing!

Certainly there are those who enjoy jumping on every situation, "firing from the hip." But while that might give the odd adrenaline rush, it is not necessarily an effective practice. Most of us enjoy some sensible pressure and often feel that we perform best under these circumstances. What happens, though, if that pressure becomes permanent? It either becomes normal so that it ceases to have the motivational effect, or it puts us into stress overload, resulting in burnout. Neither is effective.

There are, in most jobs, a series of routine tasks that must be done regularly—read the mail, check and sign the expenses, prepare the monthly report, and so on. These tasks are usually fairly boring. Some of us look for any excuse to do something far more interesting and enjoyable, and reacting to incoming demands can seem a justifiable way of avoiding mundane tasks. . . . "Sorry, I didn't finish the report because I spent most of the day helping Jane with that computer problem." The truth is, we enjoyed dealing with the problem more than writing the report, so the routine task of writing the report suffered.

However, you can get to everything that needs to be done by spending the first ten minutes of your working day dividing tasks into two areas: tasks you *must* do and tasks you would *like to* do, if there is time.

If appropriate, plan to do the routine (boring) items first. Having completed those, reward yourself with something interesting or enjoyable.

DEALING WITH OFFICE POLITICS AND INTERRUPTIONS

It's the 80:20 rule yet again . . . 80 percent of our interruptions are caused by 20 percent of the people.

Have you ever been sitting at your desk and seen a team member heading in your direction and thought, "Oh no. Not you, not today.

Please!" That person arrives, grabs the nearest chair, takes up a comfy position, and ... you know you are in for a long session!

The difficulty is that until this team member starts to talk, you have no idea how important the subject is. If it is urgent or important, the interruption is valid. However, what do you do if this employee wants to discuss a recent vacation or their grandkid, but you have to finish preparing for a presentation that is due in ten minutes?

The answer is simple: As that person approaches your desk, stand up. For most people, your body language will convey that sitting in the visitor's chair is inappropriate at this time. At most the person might perch on the corner of your desk for a short period, but that's not a particularly comfortable spot and gives them an incentive to leave. You can then say something along the lines of "Morning, David. What can I do for you?" David's reply should tell you what you need to know. You can then invite him to sit down or suggest talking later.

Office politics and organizational matters can also wreak havoc with time management. Workday parties celebrating birthdays, promotions, and other events, even company-wide meetings that deal with general policy matters can all throw a wrench into your well-planned day. If possible, stay for a few minutes, then excuse yourself, unless the meeting is essential to the performance of your job or your role as a manager. If the meeting is about organizational restructuring, for instance, employees will have questions, and you'll need to be available to answer them.

Even though most of us play office politics in one form or another, remember you have control of your level of involvement. You can stand around the water cooler and chat, or you can bring your own bottled water and get your work done.

Still another time issue facing managers is what's known as "monkey jumping." This occurs when an employee or associate plops himself down, relates a problem (a monkey on his back, so to speak), and expects it to become yours—that is, he transfers the monkey from his back to yours!

Savvy managers should take care of the "monkey" right on the spot, suggesting ways for the problem to be solved and if appropriate, requesting feedback on any actions taken as a result of their suggestion(s).

EXPECT THE UNEXPECTED

Consider a recent daily plan and ask yourself whether you completed it. If you only did most or some of it, why was that?

The most likely reason your plan was wrecked was because of unexpected demands on your time. "Hold on though," you may say. "I can't plan for the unexpected, can I?" In fact, you can.

Ask yourself how much work you actually planned to do in eight hours. Many daily plans appear to allocate something close to eight hours of work to be done in an eight-hour day. In other words, there's no leeway for the unexpected, and when it does arise, the plan is disrupted. How realistic is it to plan eight full hours of work during an eight-hour day?

One to two hours—maybe more—of your day are likely to be spent "putting out fires." You can't plan for the actual tasks that arise, but you can allocate time for the unexpected! Keep a log for a few days to see how much time you spend on unforeseen tasks.

Once you get an average figure, allow for it in your daily plans. Suppose that handling unanticipated issues takes two hours each day. This means you should plan for about six hours' worth of work. Although such planning is an inexact science, you are more likely to accomplish the designated tasks because you've set them within a more realistic time frame.

CREATIVE PROBLEM SOLVING

Steps to a Solution

The most common term for "problem" in current corporate-speak is "issue," which sort of bubble-wraps itself around the situation to make it seem less harsh. (Sometimes a problem is also referred to as a "challenge.")

For example, if someone says, "I have some issues with that," he'll likely get a less negative or defensive reaction than if he bluntly states, "I have a problem with that." Right off the bat, the word *problem* can raise red flags.

Imagine you have a problem with your computer. Let's say you call customer service, guns blazing and angry about the particular situation. What happens? More likely than not, you'll discover that the rep on the line won't be very willing to help you and might not offer you a satisfactory solution. However, what do you think might happen if you approach the same rep tactfully, in team mode ("This situation is a real mess and I'd like to see if you can help me")? Chances are the rep will be more than willing to help you and will provide a satisfactory solution. The same is true of your employees. The trick is to maintain a sense of perspective and "cool," especially before you have all the facts (usually easier done in the workplace than when dealing with customer service representatives).

In handling a problem or issue, take the tack that you need to know why something is happening in order to reinforce it (if it is positive) or correct it (if it is negative). If you take action without knowing the cause, you may get a reaction that has nothing to do with what's actually going on. Assume nothing until you have all the facts.

CLEARLY SEPARATE
CAUSE FROM EFFECT

Cause analysis has, by definition, to deal with cause and effect. Sometimes people do not separate cause and effect, or become so confused that they attempt to deal with the effect rather than the cause.

The problem is that a cause can itself be an effect of an even deeper cause. Where, then, do you stop? The following might help to illustrate the difficulty:

- The oil burner at home breaks down, which was caused by ...
- The oil pump malfunctioning, which was caused by ...
- Faulty wiring, which was caused by ...
- The electrician not putting in correct wiring, which was caused by ...
- Poor training of the electrician, and so on.

As you can see, replacing the pump is dealing with the effect, and it would solve the problem only temporarily until the wiring went again. That is, only doing our top action in this case is too superficial. Yet dropping all the way to the bottom of the list is an equally ineffective strategy for solving this problem—you probably can't do much about that electrician's training! The most practical solution, therefore, is to ask a qualified electrician to rewire the system, and then replace the pump.

Thus the logical question is: "How far do I need to go back to solve this problem for all practical purposes?" To arrive at an answer you'll need clarity as to where your responsibility ends and others' begins. Having that, you can identify those causes of problems upon which you can take, or initiate, some form of action.

BUILD UPON A SOLID STARTING POINT

When looking at a deviation from normal, having a good set of starting blocks—that is, a sound basis to begin from—is essential. All too often we generalize far too easily. We even give titles to some of our bigger or longer-term problems: the invoicing issue, the sales dispute, the absentee problem, and so on. Everyone believes they know what is meant by each term, but often individuals have very different views that don't always match. Take the invoicing issue, for example. One administrator might see it as a need for a more motivated staff to process the invoices more quickly, while the invoicing manager might view it as a requirement for better computer facilities. The sales manager regards it as the reason why the invoices are often incorrect, while the invoicing clerk looks upon it as management expecting the impossible.

Setting the starting blocks correctly helps an athlete avoid false or bad starts. The same applies with cause analysis: If the right start is made, the rest becomes easier and you don't have to make up for lost time or correct mistakes.

Before beginning any detailed analysis find out exactly what deviation you are trying to analyze and ask:

- What or who is involved?
- Exactly what is the deviation from normal?

By applying these questions to the aforementioned invoicing issue, for instance, you can track the processes that invoices go through and discover which ones are late. Thus you will begin to define the cause of the problem.

Deviations can also be positive, so you can apply the same principles to define the starting blocks for those as well.

DEFINE THE PROBLEM EFFECTIVELY, AND BE SPECIFIC

"Effectively" means being systematic about collecting relevant information. Your first impulse might be to jot down everything you know about the issue—data, probable causes, more data, possible actions, and so forth, all mixed up together. However, by doing this you might be jumping the gun.

Cause analysis must be systematic, otherwise you run the danger of going down blind alleys only to find—sometimes much later—that you have to return to the main route. Moreover, there is little point in trying to check a possible cause until you have some facts against which to judge whether it is the real reason for the deviation or not.

First, decide if you already know why the issue exists. If you are absolutely sure you know the cause, then you don't need cause analysis.

If you don't know or are unsure why the issue exists, use the following to guide you in systematically collecting data about it. Ask:

- What is happening?
- When does it happen?

- How does it show up?
- Where is it happening?
- Who is involved?

When collecting data about the deviation (good or bad), people tend to generalize. Suppose, for example, there is a problem with invoices going out late. Questions you have already asked might generate the following answers:

- What?—invoices
- Why?—not too sure, might be the computer
- When?—this quarter
- How?—at management meeting
- Where?—accounts department
- Who?—accounts staff

This information is too general to be of much practical use, so delve deeper by asking specific, pointed questions. If you are trying to get information from others who are generalizing, try adding the word *exactly* to each question:

- What (exactly)?—all invoices for furniture over $1,500 going out ten days late
- Why (exactly)?—the cause is unknown
- When (exactly)?—since March 1 of this year
- How (exactly)?—reported by invoicing section leader at meeting on March 30
- Where (exactly)?—invoicing section, accounts department
- Who (exactly)?—only those staff in the section who deal with furniture invoices over $1,500

USE CHARTS AND DIAGRAMS TO HELP

When trying to define a problem, words alone can be restrictive. Sometimes it is difficult to discern what is happening, or where, using only words. We have all heard the phrase "One picture is worth a thousand words." In the case of cause analysis, a picture or diagram can also save a thousand words!

A chart or diagram can further help to define the problem because they can include additional information. Not only will these visual aids help you clearly delineate who has done what, but they also can help you sort information into relevant clusters of data. For instance, a bar graph can show the varying rates of product return from month to month, allowing you to determine if there is a trend that must be addressed.

Other types of useful charts are:

- Line graph—depicts the connection between two sets of data, one represented vertically and the other, horizontally. The relationship is defined where the two scales intersect.
- Bar chart—similar to a graph, but with shaded blocks instead of a plotting line.
- Pie chart—shows data in proportion to one another.
- Frequency list—counts the number of times an activity occurs so that the daily/weekly/monthly frequency can be identified.

Pictorial depictions can also help you spot trends as well as provide you with a different point of view, and can give you insights that you might otherwise miss.

AVOID ASSUMPTIONS, ESPECIALLY WHEN DEALING WITH PEOPLE

In his book, *The Four Agreements*, Don Miguel Ruiz advises against making assumptions in any situation. He provides an example of encountering someone you have a crush on at the mall. The person smiles at you and walks away, giving you a sense that she likes you back. That encounter might cause you to create an entire relationship that in fact may only exist in your mind.

This example applies to the workplace as well. By assuming that X person always reacts in a certain way or is at the bottom of particular problem, you are merely assigning blame, rather than dealing with the facts.

Ruiz recommends dealing with assumptions by asking questions. "Have the courage to ask questions until you are clear as you can be, and even then do not assume you know all there is to know about a given situation," he writes. Of course, you can't check everything. But if you make assumptions, make sure they are credible; that is, they have at least some basis in hard facts.

Cause analysis relies on facts, so identify any assumptions in the data and check to see whether they are correct. On occasions where you cannot verify a given point, mark the data in some way to show that it is an assumption rather than fact.

DEVIATIONS ARE CAUSED BY CHANGES

Having collected the data, you now need to try and identify possible causes of the problem. For any deviation there could be many possibilities. For starters, you might want to look at the changes that have occurred in the categories of human resources, machinery or systems, and methods or procedures. Then you might look into the inputs of the process, such as raw materials. How the work comes to a group should also be examined.

You might hold a personal or group brainstorming-type session to generate various possibilities, asking: "What could possibly cause this situation?"

The resulting list can be enormous, and it might take a long time to check each one. What is needed is some concept or method that reduces the list of possibilities to those likely to have a direct bearing on the problem.

This is where Newton's first law of motion comes in. The law states: "Every body continues in a state of rest or uniform motion in a straight line unless acted upon by an external impressed force." This concept—that most things go along uninterrupted until some outside force comes along and disturbs it—is the real key to effective cause analysis. Say, for example, my cat Savannah is sleeping (at rest) on my desk. I reach over and pet her (an external force), causing her to wake up and move. The cause of the effect is readily evident in this case. Finding solutions to workplace problems is seldom this straightforward, though the logic is the same.

Try to identify what relevant changes have occurred at or around the time the deviation first arose. It will also help to note when the change occurred. Then you can generate possible causes from these changes. For example, suppose there was a change in the computer system. The possible cause might be: "The new computer system is faulty, making incorrect calculations."

FINDING THE REAL OR
UNDERLYING CAUSE

Now you have a list of possible causes. It is fairly unlikely that they all caused the deviation, but how do you decide which causes are at the bottom of the issue?

A problem-solving group can be divided into subgroups, where each subgroup takes a possible cause to check on and report back. This represents a logical division of labor, but you must determine if it is really necessary to spend a lot of time modifying everything to see the effect. The question is how to determine this.

Other groups might pick the particular cause they like the look of and go off to remedy that. This might be fine, provided they have chosen the right cause. But do you know how much time and money will be wasted if it's not the right one?

What is needed is some method of "eliminating the impossible," as Sherlock Holmes would say.

"How often have I said to you that when you have eliminated the impossible, whatever remains, however improbable, must be the truth?"

—Sir Arthur Conan Doyle, *The Sign of the Four*

Take each of the possible causes and compare each one with the "what, why, when, how, where, and who" data you collected. Ask whether that cause would explain all of the facts you have. For example, let's say one possible cause is "a glitch in the new computer system." Using your data you might discover that the system was changed *after* the problem first arose. This finding eliminates that cause!

When you have eliminated the impossible causes via this approach, whatever is left must be the truth, or at least pretty close to it.

What if you eliminate everything? Either one or more of your facts are wrong, or you have missed a change somewhere along the line.

WHEN THERE MAY BE MORE THAN ONE CAUSE

Consider the following problem: *Production of car components has fallen by 20 percent.* After cause analysis, the production manager is left with several possible causes that cannot be entirely eliminated:

- Faulty batch of raw material (metal rods) delivered.
- Quality standards (tolerances on dimensions) now more stringent, causing more scrap.
- Reduced productivity due to unfounded rumors of an unfriendly takeover.
- Increased checking by Quality Control, increasing reject rate.

It might help to prioritize action by asking the following questions:

- Which is the root *cause*—the one that directly produces the problem?
- Which are *contributory causes*—those that contribute to the problem but do not directly cause it?

In the example, the root cause is more stringent quality standards, which are found to be unrealistic for the relatively old machines in the factory. Consequently, production of "good" components fell by 20 percent. The other factors contributed to the problem but did not actually cause it. The rumors of a takeover were a direct result of uncertainty engendered by the reduced production output, while the faulty material only applied to one day's production. The higher reject rates meant more frequent checking by the inspectors.

When investigating multiple causes, remember to follow the thread of events and keep asking questions until you find the single, major contributing factor. In this case, all roads lead back to the outdated machinery, and the fact that it could not produce components that met updated standards.

SOUND DECISION-MAKING

Choosing the Right Option

Logical decisions are those with a finite number of options. Your objective is to select the options that best meet the requirement. For example, choosing a new computer system falls into this category as would deciding who to promote or recruit.

The wrong choice would cause problems. The more important the decision, the greater the problems that arise from a wrong choice. Imagine the costs (direct and indirect) of recruiting the wrong person.

Creative decisions are those that address problems without obvious solutions, so you must create them. Having generated possible options, you can then evaluate the problem or issue in much the same way as you would with a logical decision. Decisions that fall into this category might include how to market services more widely or how to increase revenue.

Creative decisions encourage novel approaches and ideas, and they are vital in finding new and innovative ways to move forward.

SET CRITERIA BEFORE THINKING ABOUT THE OPTIONS

Think about a recent decision and how you went about making it. You probably started by weighing various options and then comparing them to decide which one best suited your purposes. Although this method can be effective, unbeknownst to you your decision may have been *biased*.

Have you ever convinced yourself that something is the best option solely because you liked that particular choice? In fact, you may well have made up your mind unconsciously after seeing the one you liked. The rest were effectively a lost cause. In cases like this, it's easy to "bend" the requirements to suit our bias—without even realizing it. For example, a friend went out to buy a minivan and came back with a two-seat sports car. His partner suggested he might need to buy a roof rack to make room for his three kids. After a couple of weeks he traded in the car for the minivan, but it cost him (in more ways than one)!

Everyone has biases; it's part of being human. You can, however, avoid biases that create bad choices by setting some criteria before even considering any options. Criteria should describe the ideal you are trying to achieve. It helps to categorize these criteria as either "essential" or "desirable." For instance, if you are leasing office space, some of the criteria might be: appeal to customers and cost per square foot (essential), and proximity to public transportation and length of the lease (desirable). It is perfectly fine to include likes and dislikes in your criteria, provided they are appropriate (and legal).

CONSIDER A RANGE OF OPTIONS, INCLUDING DO NOTHING

Another aspect of potential bias is when you unreasonably limit the options to the one or two that you like, or you default to options that have worked before. Except for "yes/no" decisions, there are rarely only just a couple of options.

A manifestation of this problem is when you hear yourself (or someone else) saying, "But we have always done it this way." Fear of the unknown can easily generate unreasonable bias against new or different approaches to doing things.

"If you have a workforce that enjoys each other, they trust each other, they trust management, they're proud of where they work—then they're going to deliver a good product."

—Jeff Smisek, former CEO, Continental Airlines

At the other end of the scale, some decision-making discussions never consider the option of "Stay as we are." The way forward should represent an improvement on the current position. If you don't consider the current position, how can you measure improvement? And if it isn't broken, why fix it?

Look at the options being generated, including the option of "Stay as we are," and ask yourself whether they represent a reasonable range.

CONSIDER THE RISKS AND BENEFITS

Most people look at the benefits of available options when trying to make a decision. Some, however, seem to feel that considering the risks introduces a negative note to the proceedings. Consequently, the risks receive little, if any, attention. In some work environments people find that suggesting risks is unacceptable, so they keep quiet about them.

At the opposite end of the spectrum are those who only opt for "safe" decisions, that is, those that seem to carry minimum risk. While such decisions might seem secure, the question should be: "Will the low-risk option actually produce the best result?" There might be another, better option that has higher (though manageable) risks but that might deliver far greater benefits.

Good decision-making considers both the benefits and the risks of each option. The perfect option has yet to be invented. Try to consider the severity and likelihood of the risk so as to indicate its significance.

Consider the issue of leasing office space (a pretty common problem for businesses). Option A might be near public transportation, be visually appealing to customers, and have a low cost per square foot (attributes that all score high on the benefit scale); and it might have a short-term lease (making it low on the risk scale). Conversely, Option B may lack visual appeal, have a high cost per square foot, and not be near public transportation (attributes that score low on the benefit scale). Even if it had the same short-term lease (making both options equal on the risk scale), Option A is preferable.

Decision-making is a balancing act—weighing the benefits of each option against the risks. If there is an option with the highest benefits and least snags, the decision is easy. If, on the other hand, there is a high-benefit/high-risk option, ask whether it is possible to reduce or manage those risks in order to achieve the benefits.

EFFECTIVE GROUP DECISION-MAKING

Group decision-making can become highly emotional. One person wants Approach A; someone else is strongly in favor of Approach B. Tempers may flare when the two opposing viewpoints clash. It can turn into a power struggle, which benefits no one.

A way to circumvent this is to have each side present its case to the group, with the goal of finding a satisfactory solution (see the chapter on creative problem solving). You can do this via black/white boards, PowerPoint presentations, flip charts, or any method that effectively presents the salient points of each party. Ask each individual to give you their respective views, and summarize them for presentation to the entire group. Each will have his uninterrupted time to describe his position using the appropriate method of presentation. That way, the pros and cons of each viewpoint will be enumerated, and a decision will be based on the facts—what makes most sense for the team and the organization. Such an approach invests the entire group in the decision. It is no longer about the person but the situation.

Healthy disagreement is fine and should be encouraged as long as all participants stick to facts and avoid finger pointing and accusations. If you feel that a more personal argument is about to erupt, then it's best to call a "time out." If an immediate decision is not called for, suggest that opposing parties gather pertinent information and present it at a later date.

DECIDING ON THE BASIS OF BENEFITS VERSUS SNAGS

If you ask most people how they make decisions, they will usually say something like: "I weigh up the benefits of the options, do the same with the snags, then choose."

If everyone uses the same decision-making processes, then why do we differ so much in our choices? Most of us have attended meetings where someone was vehemently opposed to the option we wanted, or supported an option that we would never choose. Most put this down to differences in "individual judgments." Each person believes that his or her reasoning is right. But the truth is, it's more about opinion.

When weighing up benefits versus snags, people seem to err toward one side or the other. Someone with a "glass half empty" (pessimistic) standpoint will see the snags as more significant than the benefits, whereas the person with the "glass half full" (optimistic) view will see benefits as more significant than risks. Thus they will probably favor different options.

As a manager you'll need to find a mutually acceptable way of objectively evaluating both the benefits and the snags of the options via a scoring scale or a "high, medium, or low" rating. Remember, though, that the figures are only an expression of your collective judgment. These methods seem to work far better than emotional arguments borne of frustration, especially when people feel compelled to defend their reasoning and judgments.

YOU WILL NEVER HAVE ALL OF THE INFORMATION. DECIDE!

Making the decision itself is often one of the hardest moments a manager can face. Some people are prepared to take risks that accompany decision-making, others are not. However, one question all managers ask is: "Do I have all the information I need?"

Some people want to dot every "i" and cross every "t" before they decide anything. They do this in order to reduce the chances of being wrong. However, this is not only impossible but impractical. How often do you have all the information you would like? We can rarely be certain of every fact, and so many decisions are based on at least some assumptions.

People understandably want to make the right decision, but they need to accept they won't get every little bit of data they would like. The question should then be rephrased to: "Do I have all the essential information to make a reasoned decision?" Decisions are often concerned to some extent with predicting the future, and some assumptions are therefore inevitable.

If you could guarantee that all your decisions were right, you would likely be at least a millionaire! (But so would everyone else, having figured out the same technique.) All you can hope to do is be successful with the important decisions you make. Since some errors are inevitable, no manager should expect perfection in decision-making.

When a decision is needed, failure to decide can be a far bigger problem than making a wrong decision. It's like the slogan from the 1960s, "Not to decide is to decide."

STIMULATING CREATIVITY

The Value of Brainstorming

Although many of the decisions you and members of your team make will seem quick and easy, others will require a more creative process. While some decisions and ideas will necessarily originate with individual team members, others can flow from group activity. This is where the activity known as "brainstorming" comes in.

Brainstorming isn't necessary or appropriate for every decision. Probably 80 percent of our decisions fall into the category of quick decisions. Someone asks if she can have tomorrow off or if he can borrow the computer for a couple of hours. There are people who would give each issue detailed consideration, but most of us simply react immediately to these everyday requests and use a "gut feeling" to make a decision. In other words, your decision seems naturally right at the time.

However, quick decisions do not have to mean "instant." There is usually some thinking time, even if only a minute or two. Often the options are simple: either a "yes" or "no."

Perhaps more so than other types of workers, managers need to school themselves to consider two questions before making even small decisions. They must ask:

1. What are the essential criteria?
2. What are the main risks on both options?

Suppose, for example, someone asks to borrow your computer for the afternoon. Before automatically answering either way, you think:

- I can finish the vital report for the board by lunchtime (Criteria).
- "Yes" means I won't have computer access (Risk A), but since I'll be calling on customers I won't likely need it.
- "No" means I would possibly be seen as unhelpful (Risk B).

In this situation, the ramifications of Risk B—being seen as unhelpful—outweigh those of Risk A, which is that although you need the computer sometimes, such is not the case this afternoon. Conclusion: Agree to the request.

You might already unconsciously do something like this. But asking yourself those two quick questions before making even small decisions should help you circumvent the consequences of inaction (the "deadline" passes, and with it all of the attendant problems) or a too-rapid "gut reaction" (you want to be nice, but you did need the computer after all and now you'll be behind on your work) that causes more problems than it solves.

Now let's move on to more complicated decisions. Often these decisions have big implications for the team or even for the organization as a whole. These are the decisions for which you want to get buy-in from the entire group.

BRAINSTORMING AS A CREATIVE METHOD

Everyone can be creative, but some seem to find it easier than others. People often seem to link creativity with personality traits: for example, "creative people are extroverts." While introverts may be more reluctant to suggest zany solutions in a group, personality type may not be the reason for an apparent lack of creativity. Instead it may be due to a thinking style.

Certain people mentally screen out ideas by considering the criteria too early. For example, "I have this idea but the cost would probably be too high, so I won't suggest it." Consequently a potentially useful solution has been lost. Why, then, is it potentially useful even if it's too expensive? After all, someone might suggest a way of reducing the cost of this solution while retaining the chief benefit. But this cannot be done if the idea is never suggested.

Do not set (or even discuss) any criteria before or during a brainstorming session whose purpose is to generate options. At this stage the objective is quantity, rather than quality, of ideas.

Explain to your team that the aim of the brainstorming session is to generate outside-the-suggestion-box ideas and options, no matter how far-fetched they may initially sound. The more practical criteria will be discussed later. Reward them for their creativity by encouraging their suggestions.

THE PITFALLS OF EVALUATING DURING BRAINSTORMING

Some participants might try to impulsively evaluate proposed ideas during a brainstorming session and say things such as:

- "Hold on, Jane. That idea won't be acceptable to the board."
- "The workshop won't be able to do that, Harry."
- "Oh, come on, be realistic, Dave. There's not enough time for that."

Comments like these will kill creativity very quickly, especially among those who are more reluctant to suggest new and different options, or with quieter people who might also lack confidence. They feel they are being quite brave to suggest something in the first place and will simply clam up in the face of such comments. Even the most thick-skinned person will soon give up if he must deal with ongoing negativity. As a result, the number of ideas will be significantly reduced.

Set a clear rule at the onset—no evaluation of others' ideas (yet). Explain why this is so important and stress that the ideas will be evaluated, but later. You might even nominate one of the team as a monitor who will stop the meeting immediately if the rule is breached.

Some people do not even realize that they are evaluating. You can help the inadvertent (and frequent) offender stop this behavior. With a smile, try making a light joke of it: "There you go again, Fred."

ENCOURAGE IDEAS OUTSIDE THE SUGGESTION BOX—HAVE SOME FUN!

Creative or novel ideas are best nurtured in a friendly, positive, and enthusiastic atmosphere. People are more willing to open up and share their innermost feelings when they have a sense of relaxation and freedom. This is why corporate retreats and "character building" sessions have become so popular—new and different facets of a person appear once outside the 9-to-5 setting. By taking you out of your zone of expectation, the situation encourages you to come up with new ideas or ways of operating.

Of course it's impractical (and expensive) to set every brainstorming session at a retreat. But if the atmosphere is serious and businesslike, people will have a tendency to play it safe and only propose tried and tested ideas that have been known to work in the past. So how do you create a mood conducive to thinking outside the suggestion box?

According to human resources consultant Rafe Harwood, four things are essential to a good brainstorming session:

- Criticism is ruled out—no matter how strange the idea
- Freewheeling is welcomed—let imagination run as free as possible
- Quantity is wanted—generate as many ideas as possible
- Combination and improvement are sought—building on ideas of other members

Good brainstorming sessions can be done anywhere, even in the cafeteria or a meeting room. Encouraging humor and laughter is also effective in generating new ideas, as long as people are laughing with—and not at—each other. Effective managers will take notice of the difference, and circumvent the latter by pointing out the inappropriateness of making fun of others.

Out of maybe twenty suggestions there is often one gem that can be modified, but the other nineteen are needed to encourage it in the first place.

DELEGATE, DELEGATE, DELEGATE!

Trust Your Employees

Delegation is entrusting part of your job as a manager (specific activities or decisions) to a member of your team and giving them the responsibility and authority to carry it out. However, as a manager you, rather than the employee, are ultimately accountable and answerable for the activity.

The act of delegation must be separated from simply issuing work. *Issuing work* means deciding which member of the team should carry out some task that is part of their normal role anyway. Delegation, on the other hand, involves giving someone a task that is normally part of the manager's job.

Effective delegation is important for the following reasons:

- It enables the manager to spend time on more important tasks.
- It's an excellent way of developing people who wish to advance in the organization.
- It is highly motivational—although, if done badly, the reverse can also true.

PICK THE RIGHT TASK

Some managers believe they are delegating when in fact all they are doing is issuing work that would normally be done by a member of the team anyway.

Others consider delegating part of their job, but then the only tasks that seem to be delegated are those that the manager can't be bothered to do personally. Still other managers only delegate when they are in "work overload," as in, "Mavis, would you finish off the figures on my monthly report for me? I have to go to that section meeting now and won't have time to do them."

To delegate effectively, determine which tasks to select. Make an initial list of all the main tasks you perform. Then ask yourself which would be worth delegating for the following reasons:

- It would save you valuable time.
- It might motivate a member of the team.
- It would help develop someone's skills and/or knowledge.

Now that you have identified those tasks that you could delegate, you need to find the right person to delegate to.

PICK THE RIGHT PERSON

You can probably think of at least one member of your team whom you would immediately consider as a prime candidate. Such people are usually experienced and need very little briefing from you. Plus, they always offer to help in a crisis. Every manager needs—or would like—someone like that on her team. The danger is that such a person will take on too much. Overload a willing horse, and even it is likely to collapse!

Some managers never consider delegating anything to an inexperienced or new member of the team because they assume, perhaps subconsciously, that no experience signifies a lack of ability. How, then, do you go about choosing the right person for the task?

First, ask yourself *why* you are considering delegating this particular task. Now think about the skill and knowledge requirements of the task, and then consider the individual strengths and needs of the people on your team in this particular field (previous discussion at appraisal or review meetings should help here).

Next, try to match the task requirements to the individual strengths and needs. Remember, do not assume lack of experience means no ability—sometimes someone with less experience takes a fresh approach to the job and can do it even more efficiently than someone with more direct experience. And also consider how the added work will affect the productivity and schedule of the trusted team member.

Once you feel you've chosen the right person, set a specific objective: for example, "Develop Andrew's financial control skills and knowledge within three months by delegating production of the monthly 'budget versus spend' report to him."

PICK THE RIGHT CHALLENGE

Make sure your perception of a challenge is commensurate with that of your team members. Consider the following example:

Karen (the manager): "Dawn, I need your help. I've just been told that I'm going on a management course next week and we've got to purchase some additional computers. I was scheduled to put together a proposal and discuss it with the director. Since I'm going away, and you're my right-hand person, I'd like you to take a crack at it."

Dawn (the assistant, trying to keep the panic out of her voice): "Thanks for thinking of me, Karen, but I have never put a proposal together; much less tried to persuade a director with one! I'm not at all sure that I could do that . . . I have no idea how to prepare a presentation, let alone give one."

Karen: "Everyone has to start somewhere. I had to do that sort of thing when I was in your position eighteen months ago. My predecessor used to believe in throwing people in at the deep end, and that's how I learned. This will be a good challenge for you. There's nothing like a meeting with a director to focus the mind. I'm sure you'll cope if you give it a try."

Dawn (anxious to leave the office because she wants to find a more experienced team member to help bail her out): "Well, I sincerely doubt it . . . and you won't even be here to even provide guidance."

How do you think Dawn will fare? What is seen by Karen as a challenge is seen by Dawn as impossible. Because you can do something (or could when you were in a team member's job) does not mean someone else can. After all, everyone has different abilities, goals, and talents.

Before deciding to delegate a task to a particular team member, ask yourself if he has (or can develop, in the time available) the knowledge and/or skills, as well as the confidence, to cope with the task. If you are unsure, you might want to sit down and discuss the possibility with him so as to discern how he feels about it. Alternatively, you might want the potential delegatee to "ride shotgun" with you before formally handing over responsibility. Leaving the employee in charge when you're out for a day allows for a trial run. If after that, the team member still sees the task as impossible, consider giving the task to someone else.

TRUST PEOPLE

Give Them the Authority They Need

Some managers seem altogether too happy to delegate responsibility to team members but never give them the authority to do the job properly. In this context, *authority* is defined as the power to make independent decisions. Failure to delegate effectively probably stems from fear. However, it is extremely frustrating if a team member keeps running to you, the manager, every time a decision on even the most minor aspects of a delegated job is needed.

So how do you delegate the authority without relinquishing control or abdicating responsibility altogether? The answer is simple: allow the team member to make independent decisions within certain limitations. Setting limits will help avoid disasters.

For example, suppose you delegate the task of negotiating a price with an important customer. The team member will probably ask, "How far can I go?" to which you might reply: "We have quoted $90,000 for one module. Now they may find they need two and therefore want to negotiate. You can negotiate a discount of up to 10 percent—that gives a minimum price of $178,200 for two modules—or a lower discount and free maintenance worth $3,000, whichever you think most appropriate at the time. If they insist on a deal that would take us below the minimum price of $178,200, check with me before agreeing to anything."

This allows the team member some leeway for decision-making but prevents him from making costly—and serious—mistakes.

WHEN BORING TASKS ARE JUST THAT

Sometimes a manager wants to "dress up" a boring task before delegating it. The manager will say: "Something very important has cropped up Andrea, which I think you will find interesting. The board wants an analysis of our sales over the last year by product and geographical district. You will have to prepare analyses one day, so how about starting now?"

What the manager means, however, is this: "Andrea, I'm strapped for time, and our director is screaming for information. For the next couple of hours, I'll call out figures, and you punch the calculator and feed me the answers. By the way, I haven't the time to actually explain any of it at the moment!"

Not only do many managers make a habit of this deceptive approach, but they also think their victims actually believe what they tell them! Of course, the victim catches on quickly, so when the manager says he has "an interesting job," Andrea knows something boring or mundane is imminent. Sooner (usually) or later, people see through such deception, intentional or otherwise.

If you need help with a boring but necessary task, say so up front. If you balance it by delegating interesting and challenging work, most team members will be prepared to help with even the most routine jobs.

ENCOURAGE PEOPLE
TO DO THE PLANNING!

Some managers believe delegation involves telling team members what is required, exactly how it should be carried out, and by when. They usually offer the following rationale:

1. "Well, I've done the job umpteen times before and so I know the best way."
2. "They don't know how to do the job, since they've never done it before."

However, these are incorrect assumptions. Say you've done a task many times. Does that mean you know the best or the only way of doing it? Of course not. Sometimes the person who tackles the job for the first time comes up with a new method that is even more effective than what had been used for months or even years before.

Whatever the task, a plan is needed to show who needs to do what and by when. Rather than suggest the plan, ask your team members how they would tackle the task. Then decide whether their method would achieve the objective. If it will work (even though it may differ from your approach), let them do it their way, because they will be more committed to their course of action. Provide advice only if a basic flaw appears in their plan or if they have no idea how to go about the task.

ENCOURAGE PEOPLE TO CHECK IN, AND GIVE THEM ACCESS

When considering whether to delegate a task, managers sometimes fear that they will lose control. They think, "If I delegate this task, I'm not doing it, so I'm not in control of it." Attempting to overcome this perceived difficulty, the manager sets up frequent review dates to meet with the team member and see how things are going. If the team member does not show up for some of these meetings, the manager might wonder why and start to develop delegator's twitch.

Suddenly the manager is constantly looking over the team member's shoulder, asking how things are going. Rather than finding this helpful or supportive, the team member usually sees this, often correctly, as interference or distrust.

So how do you maintain some control without interfering or showing distrust of the person to whom you have delegated the work? First, encourage the employee to suggest checkpoints—that is, the stages in the task when you should step in and do a quick review. She will likely come up with the same points you would have, but now it's her brainchild, not your interference. Second, allow her access to you if she wants to discuss any aspects of the task: "I have given you the job because I know you can do it. Rather than have me constantly check on you, if you want to discuss anything, just come and talk to me." She now knows that she can get any information she wants at any time and has been given the impetus to do so.

EVERYONE MAKES MISTAKES— ESPECIALLY WHEN THEY'RE LEARNING

Delegation can at first be rather like learning to drive: horrible crunching of gears, stalling at traffic lights, forgetting to signal occasionally, and maybe even a few near-misses. Gradually the learner becomes proficient and more skilled and experienced, and the problems fade away.

Very few people have the knack of doing an unfamiliar job perfectly the first time. Most managers realize this, and so to help, they become very specific about what they want and exactly how it must be done. There is of course sometimes a good reason for doing this.

But if the objective is to help the person develop, then she requires room to maneuver and must be allowed the few mistakes that are inevitable as she learns.

However, some managers seem to expect perfection right from the start and tell the employee: "Do it my way exactly so that you won't make any mistakes and let me down." What sort of learning experience or development is that? The team member will hardly be able to think for herself when she must eventually make her own decisions.

Be prepared to accept a few minor mistakes while the team member develops skill and knowledge. At strategic points, jointly review her performance to find out what she has learned and what she would do differently next time.

A final note: During the discussion when you are jointly planning the task, try to anticipate and prevent any serious problems (potential disasters). Agree what actions are needed, and together work out the most effective way of monitoring them.

REALITY CHECK—HOW DO THEY FEEL ABOUT THE TASK?

Oftentimes managers neglect a very important aspect of delegation: They fail to find out how the team member *really* feels about doing the task.

Some managers explain the task and what is involved in its successful completion at considerable length, believing that a clear explanation is all that is necessary—that is, if you fully understand it, you will be prepared to do it. Their closing remark is usually something like, "Do you understand all that?" What is the team member supposed to say? The answer is likely to be a vague nod or a mumbled "S'pose so." The manager believes everything is fine. The team member might well understand the task, but that does not mean that he wants to do it.

Successful delegation requires the team member's commitment and motivation, and the only real way to discern that is by asking directly. Many times managers seem to rely on mental waves or "vibes." While some managers are certainly good at discerning team members' attitudes, the chief danger is that "vibes" can be easily misinterpreted.

So in addition to explaining or discussing the task, toward the end of your conversation ask the team member how he feels about doing the task, and listen carefully to his answer. If he appears unhappy or uneasy about the task, your instructions, or his own role, find out why. Then you and the team member can work together in dealing with the concerns.

AVOID THE BLACK HOLE—GIVE FEEDBACK WHEN IT'S DONE

Most managers monitor progress on the delegated task as it proceeds. However, once the task has been completed, a strange phenomenon seems to materialize—the "black hole."

Say a task (an important report, say) is delegated effectively, the team member is happy to do the work, and preparation of the report proceeds as planned with regular review discussions (praise for things done well and constructive discussion about any difficulties).

Eventually the report is completed successfully and left on the boss's desk.

Then what? Often, absolutely nothing! The report disappears into a "black hole" never to be seen or mentioned again.

Delegation should be a learning experience, and the most valuable learning comes from reviewing the outcome of a project after it has been completed. Yet, while there is feedback and discussion during the course of the project, a review discussion "after the fact" is extremely rare. Thus a key opportunity for positive learning—and future motivation—has been missed.

After completion of the task, agree on a date to sit down and review how the project went. Direct four questions (or your own version of them) to the team member and then discuss them:

1. How do you feel it went?
2. What went particularly well and why?
3. What difficulties did you encounter, and how did you handle them?
4. What have you learned, and how will you use the knowledge?

People like feedback if it is done constructively. The post mortem discussion should also contain a critique of the outcome as well as any feedback from superiors on content, and so forth. The discussion can be brief, and the resulting benefits will be more than worth the time spent.

MILLENNIALS: THE FACTS

1. Millennials are now the largest generation in the U.S. population.

2. Millennials have been shaped by technology.

3. Millennials value family, creativity, and community in their work.

4. Millennials stay with their first employer longer than previous generations.

Today's workforce is the most diverse it's ever been, with Millennials and Gen Xers rubbing shoulders with soon-to-retire Baby Boomers. This presents new challenges to today's managers.

Although as manager you're empowered to make decisions regarding how the team will achieve its goals, the best decisions are those in which the team has input.

At the heart of good management is building a team—people who can work together effectively, whose strengths and weaknesses balance one another, and who are motivated, enthusiastic, and creative.

Photo credit: © iStockphoto.com/annebaek

The basic rule of e-mail is: Reread before hitting "Send." Something that sounds one way in your mind may come off quite differently on the computer screen of the receiver. Take your time and read through your e-mails before you send them.

Photo credit: © iStockphoto.com/peshkov

Find out what college degree you need to advance to the next rung on your managerial career. Many companies offer tuition assistance to employees who are attending school in order to assume greater responsibilities in company management.

Photo credit: © iStockphoto.com/ Pamela Moore

Considerations of parental duties, commute distances, and other factors have contributed to a rise in the number of telecommuters. Employees work from home full time or part of the week.

Photo credit: © iStockphoto.com/Steve Debenport

Goal Setting

S specific

M measurable

A attainable

R relevant

T time – bound

Top: Many managers use the SMART method in setting team and personal goals. Whatever method you use, your goals must be clearly set out and should be quantifiable.

Bottom: A to-do list is one of a manager's most valuable tools, allowing her to prioritize tasks, allocate each one the appropriate amount of time for completion, and bring order to a busy day.

Top: Success in business comes in large part from having a clear, viable, and carefully thought-out strategy, one that can be implemented by managers and their teams.

Bottom: Charts and graphs can be a valuable help in understanding trends and explaining them clearly to others. Invest time in understanding how to create them, and use them in your presentations.

A group decision means each member of the team has to buy in on it and will feel a greater sense of commitment to carrying it out.

You have the responsibility of ensuring that your team members follow all health and safety regulations on the job, have all the proper safety equipment they may need, and are trained in all company-mandated procedures.

Creating a process isn't an end in itself; the process is a tool you fashion in order to solve a larger problem or issue. But if you don't get the process right, you probably won't achieve the goal—at least not as completely and efficiently.

Top: Questions for a job candidate should seek to find out both if the interviewee has the technical skills required and if she or he will be a good personal fit with the team.

Bottom: When terminating an employee, either as part of a layoff or for cause, it's essential to follow all the rules. Keep the process as impersonal as possible to avoid getting into a confrontation with the employee.

TURNING AROUND COUNTERPRODUCTIVE BEHAVIOR

Finding the Source of Trouble

Employees represent a significant investment on the part of companies. Though the media makes it sound like employees who mess up or hit a trouble spot are immediately fired, most companies are more interested in trying to resolve the situation to protect their investment. Companies and their managers (like you) often genuinely care about the happiness and well-being of employees.

"Good management is the art of making problems so interesting and their solutions so constructive that everyone wants to get to work and deal with them."

—Paul Hawken, American entrepreneur and environmentalist

Consistent, regular feedback is the most effective means to keep most employees on the right track when it comes to job performance and compliance with company rules and policies. Consider this an incremental process; no one makes major changes overnight. If you see a pattern of behavior emerging, focus on one facet of it at a time. If the issue is time management, you might cover the topic of establishing timelines this week and prioritizing next week. This is a work in progress, and results won't necessarily be consistent. But be patient. This is the most important kind of shaping, and it's well worth the effort and time you put into it.

Let Them Take the Initiative

Employees need to know that they really can come to you whenever they feel they need to, not just when you determine it's appropriate for them to do so. Encourage them to take the initiative in setting up meetings with you if they are concerned about something.

Sometimes inappropriate behavior at work reflects problems outside the workplace, such as at home. A spouse or child may be ill or a marriage might be breaking up. There may be financial difficulties or substance abuse. Sometimes inappropriate behavior is a warning sign of deeper personal issues, such as drug use or psychological problems. Many companies offer employee assistance program (EAP) benefits or other services to get troubled employees the help they need. Employees who have a lot of personal problems or who aren't a good fit with their jobs or work groups often end up becoming self-destructive. Clearly this is not good for them, for other employees, or for the company. Signs that this is happening include these:

- Not getting work done on time or even at all
- A generally negative attitude
- Yelling and angry outbursts
- Engaging in passive-aggressive behavior (actions that appear legitimate or helpful but really are not)
- Trying to rally other employees to side with them
- Going from cubicle to office to cubicle, stirring up trouble
- Tuning out or being argumentative at staff meetings

- Showing up late, leaving early, or taking excessively long lunches
- Staying on the phone for a long time, often on personal calls, or discussing personal matters with coworkers or customers
- Flagrantly violating or ignoring company policies

Inappropriate behavior may be nothing more than the actions of someone who doesn't really know how he or she is supposed to behave in the workplace. Sometimes the employee's work style is the primary factor in performance and production matters. And sometimes people simply have trouble finding their bearings, particularly in times of major change such as corporate restructuring. New employees as well as seasoned employees whose job responsibilities depart from previous experience might be struggling to find a good match between their personal work styles and their new job assignments.

STRIVING FOR OPTIMAL FUNCTIONING

Problems within a team can result from personal issues, system issues, or both. Sometimes the source of the problem is obvious. The design team can't complete the final drawings because the software update they need to install first is backordered from the manufacturer. The customer call center can't improve call wait times and dropped calls because there are too few lines to handle the volume of incoming calls. The production department is ready to roll, but the templates were cut wrong and the manager had to send them back to the supplier. These are clearly system problems. The people are ready and eager to do what needs to be done, but they don't have what they need to move forward.

Sometimes the part of the system that's not functioning optimally is its people. Personal issues may arise from personality conflicts or performance problems. Employees may not understand their job responsibilities, or they may not like them and so attempt to pass them off or simply not do them. People have personalities, and personalities sometimes rub the wrong way. Counterproductive behaviors can destroy even the strongest teams, sometimes in a surprising manner.

Sometimes people simply don't get along with each other. Though we like to believe that adults can put aside their differences to work toward common goals, this doesn't always happen. The challenge is to isolate the personalities that are clashing—not always as easy as it sounds—so that the individuals can try to work out their differences. In other situations, people might get along fine (or even too well) but lack the skills or the competence to do the job.

In general, ruling out system problems points the finger at people problems. Sometimes it's difficult to tell where the lines are drawn. In fact, it might be a combination of the two that is causing issues. Consider the following example.

Smith and Co.'s customer call center had a telephone tree that routed calls, no matter what time of the day or night, to an extension where a "live body" could answer the phone. The sophisticated switching circuitry relied on computerized records that identified employees as they signed on to their computer terminals. The telephone tree identified them as "live" and routed calls according to a priority structure based on job function.

For months, the customer service desk fielded complaints about calls not being answered between 8 A.M. and 11 A.M. on

Tuesdays and Thursdays. Technicians checked all the wiring, circuits, and connections. Systems analysts checked all the computer algorithms to verify personnel routings. Finally a consultant from the telephone company helped set up a process for tracing call paths. This narrowed the problem to a phone in the middle of the call-forwarding sequence. Although technicians were unable to find any equipment problems in the office or with the phone, they replaced wiring and installed a new telephone that tracked all calls that rang to it, whether or not they were answered.

Astonishingly, the new phone logged no call activity on Tuesday and Thursday mornings, even though the customer service desk continued to receive complaints. So a technician decided to sit in the office and observe. After an hour or so of sitting in silence, the technician asked the employee working in the office if the phone was always so quiet. "Of course!" he said. "I unplug it as soon as I sign in, so I can work without interruptions."

The rest of the story quickly unfolded. The employee was a temporary hire who was filling in for another employee on maternity leave. Although he had his own log-on ID, the computer station itself was registered to the employee who usually worked there. So when the temporary employee logged on to the computer, the telephone tree routed calls through the office's number because the computer showed it as "live." But the temp using the office was doing special assignments, not filling in for the employee who was on leave. He worked in three different offices during the course of a week, but this was the only one with a direct-ring phone. So he did what he thought made sense to keep calls that he couldn't handle from interrupting his work: He unplugged the phone.

So, is this both a system problem and a people problem?

WHEN PERSONALITIES COLLIDE

Getting Along with Coworkers

Friendship and liking one another at work are important to many people. So important, in fact, that some individuals will take or leave jobs on the basis of the other people who work there. You probably know who these people are in your workplace, and as a manager you have likely been called upon to mediate their problems with coworkers. These employees need to get along with their coworkers; their requirement for bonding with officemates is as much a part of their personalities as of their work styles. There's nothing wrong with this, as long as it meets their needs (and doesn't interfere with productivity, theirs or yours).

Balance Work with Friends Outside Work

You can work with people you don't particularly like and still be happy in your job. It's unrealistic to expect you'll like everyone in the group. The more friends and interests you have outside work, the easier it is to work with people you don't consider to be your friends.

Whether employees like each other or not, it's still important for them to be able to work together or to share a project. This can be a challenge (which could be the understatement of the year!). The most effective way for a manager to bring people together in collaboration and cooperation is to stay focused on the job and its tasks—what the job requires and how well the employees do or don't complete those tasks. This helps them—and you—tolerate differences in personality. It also requires outstanding communication skills and the ability to wear several hats all at once.

Employees expect managers to "protect" them, to watch out for their interests and to be involved enough to understand the personalities in the group and put protections in place to assure that equality is maintained. When this doesn't happen, employees grow resentful and frustrated. Morale slides, taking productivity with it. Sometimes the issues that drive employees away seem minor, yet they reflect an underlying problem with trust and betrayal.

Don't Force the Impossible

Attempting to get employees who don't like each other to work harmoniously together doesn't always work, despite a manager's best efforts. Putting people on project teams to force them to cooperate can backfire. Don't jeopardize other team relationships and the integrity of the project by trying to engineer the impossible.

Many managers do not want to involve themselves in issues such as these because they are uncomfortable with feelings and emotions and don't like conflict. But failing to become involved can cause tension that disrupts teamwork and productivity. Employees feel their managers don't respect them when they fail to look out for their interests (it's that manager-parent role again). You can be proactive, and avoid conflict, by building in a structure that helps employees work together.

BRINGING WORKERS TOGETHER

The workplace forces people into relationships with each other that otherwise might not exist. While they often get along just fine, sometimes there are problems. It's important for you, the manager, to always have your finger on the pulse of your team so that you'll immediately know when things are out of sorts. Once a situation escalates, it can be too late to salvage the group, at least in terms of restoring it to its previous level of collaboration and productivity.

Depending on the nature of the problem, you might meet first with the entire team or with members individually. Take action as soon as you figure out what's going on. Don't wait for the right time—the right time is now. Intervene with individuals who seem to be having personal or individual performance problems. It's usually also a good idea to meet with the group to talk about the problem in general—its nature, how it's being addressed, when you expect to see things change, what changes you expect to see, and what role, if any, other group members have in resolving it. Avoid naming individuals unless there is no other way to talk about the situation. If you must use names, be sure to focus on behaviors and events, not the people.

You Need to Consistently Monitor

It's not enough to peek in at people a few times during the day to see if things look all right. You need to consistently monitor both output and attitudes. If there are problems with either, deal with the situation right away. Such interventions are not always comfortable, but they are essential.

Put on your parent, mediator, and cheerleader hats—it's time to become a multiple personality. You need to take decisive action and at the same time help group members see each other's perspectives. Sometimes the involved member will have to transfer to another department or leave the company entirely. You might need to introduce a new communications process to force employees in complementary but competitive positions to communicate more effectively. The team might need to establish a new approval process to ensure that members know about, and have the opportunity to discuss, product or service promises before anyone makes them. And when the problem is system-based, you must be willing to stick your neck out by advocating for employees. These responses build teams and create loyalty, both among group members and toward you (and sometimes even the company). Who wouldn't want to go the extra mile for a manager who at least tries to go the extra mile for them?

MANAGING MANIPULATION

Separating Facts from Emotions

Not all is as smooth as the workflow you design. People are dynamic, always thinking and feeling something different. They may disagree with the approach you've put in place, even when they were part of developing it. Some don't intend to be disruptive; they've learned counterproductive habits through the years that are hard to change. But just as you must shape, direct, and nudge the flow of work, you need to accommodate and remedy the challenges that the behaviors of others can bring to bear.

Manipulation is one such challenge. When employees try to wiggle out of assignments, the work group's productivity is disrupted. Most manipulators learn their behavior patterns early in life, and they receive reinforcement each time they use them with success. They tend to shift into manipulator mode when conventional efforts fail to produce the desired results. Manipulative behaviors target people rather than processes and present generalities rather than specifics. They may include threats, demands, insults, and efforts to make you feel guilty. Manipulation may also take the form of compliments, kindnesses, treats, and other attempts to be ingratiating.

It is important to confront manipulation with facts and specifics. Give the person a fair opportunity to present a specific concern or complaint. "Always," "never," "everyone," "no one"—these are all terms of generality. If you can't put a finger on it, you can't do much to fix it. You must separate the facts of the concern from emotions and intent so that you can examine them in context. Be detailed and tangible. Then, break issues down into manageable components. Throughout history, armies have used this "divide and conquer" tactic with great success, and it will work for you, too. If you can engage the employee in the process of identifying components, suddenly the two of you will be on the same side.

"Employees who believe that management is concerned about them as a whole person—not just an employee—are more productive, more satisfied, more fulfilled. Satisfied employees mean satisfied customers, which leads to profitability."

—Anne M. Mulcahy, former CEO, Xerox Corporation

Keep your emotional responses in check. If the employee is in tears, hand over a tissue box—without comment. If the employee is yelling, wait for the noise to stop and then speak softly so that the person must remain quiet to hear you. If the employee is using an audience of other employees for support, ask the employee to come to your office for a private talk or give the other employees a coffee break.

If your efforts to focus on processes and solutions fail to influence the employee's behavior, summarize your response in a single sentence and repeat it each time the employee tries a new tactic. Keep the tone of your voice even, firm, and friendly—not easy, as master manipulators will see what you're doing and try to break your resolve. Think of a broken record and let your tone and the message just keep repeating.

PRODUCTIVE DISAGREEMENT

The Positive Side of Conflict

Meetings can be forums for the expression of ideas and concerns. Inevitably, different opinions collide. Each person feels strongly about his or her perspective, and the situation lands in your lap. It's time to pull out your mediator hat and put your communication skills to work to negotiate a solution that all parties can accept and respect. Effective negotiation requires both sides to come to the table with the following:

- **A common allegiance:** Working toward common goals establishes a connection defined by similarities, not differences. If nothing else, both sides work for the same company and should support the company's goals, which gives them a common mission. When both sides want to achieve the same outcomes, they're often more willing to search for common ground.
- **Mutual respect:** Despite their differences, do the parties respect each other? If so, they will be able to focus on process-oriented solutions and to separate themselves from their disagreement. Respect is the foundation for trust; people must respect each other before they can trust one another to fulfill the agreements they reach.
- **Open minds:** Each party must be willing to both talk and listen so that together they can explore possible solutions.
- **Willingness to change:** Obviously each party comes to the meeting believing its perspective is valid and correct. After listening to each other and discussing the problems, all parties must be willing to change their positions to accommodate suggested solutions.

Reaching an agreement to resolve a conflict doesn't necessarily mean that each side gets what it wants. Sometimes solutions are collaborative (all parties gain) and sometimes they involve compromise (all parties give something up). Each party must feel satisfied with the solution, or the conflict remains.

FLARING TEMPERS

People lose it sometimes. Little things add up, tensions and frustrations build. People feel powerless to control or change situations that they believe should be different but that persist because you (or someone else or another department or the company) intentionally created the circumstances. Whether there is truth to this perception doesn't matter; perceptions are reality as viewed through the ever-changing hues of emotions. And the forum of the meeting can become the place to express dissatisfaction.

Avoid Excess Emotion in Meetings

Emotions and anger, especially when pent up, may entirely derail a meeting's agenda. When it appears that things are going in this direction, you have two options. You can channel the expressed frustration as constructively as possible and reschedule the intended agenda for another meeting, or you can interrupt the dialogue, acknowledge the emotions, commit to a separate meeting to specifically address the erupting concerns, and return to the scheduled agenda. The option you choose isn't as important as maintaining control.

Anger is an unmistakable sign that a person has exceeded his or her tolerance for a situation or behavior. It is an intense and powerful blend of emotion and action that often frightens even the person who is angry. Anger tends to feed on itself. The longer the shouting continues, the more volatile the anger becomes. Such meetings can quickly devolve into shouting matches, so it's crucial to defuse anger quickly. These steps can help you regain control:

- **Intercede immediately.** Don't wait for things to become truly explosive. Often, just the fact that you become involved is enough to interrupt the cycle and start turning things around.
- **Remove the audience.** If an employee is yelling and otherwise going off in front of other employees, get him or her into an office or conference room, or ask the other employees to leave for a few minutes. Someone who loses control in front of others often feels compelled to maintain or escalate angry behaviors. Removing the audience gives the angry person the freedom to back down without losing face and to regain composure.
- **Separate the behavior from the person, and request that the behavior change immediately.** Look away from the person to give him or her a few moments to pull it together, but stay in the room (unless you fear for your safety). By staying in the room, you make it clear that you're willing to do what you can to work things out and also cut short any approach that uses anger as a manipulative behavior.
- **Be an active listener.** Let the person fully explain his or her position and frustration, even if you think you already know the problem or have heard it before. Until the full story is out, ask questions only to clarify details.

- **Ask what solutions the employee would like to see.** If one or more of the employee's suggestions make sense, discuss with the employee how best to implement changes. If the suggestions don't make sense, provide a brief and factual explanation and offer an alternative.
- **Reiterate any agreements, and establish a plan to follow up.** This formalizes the arrangement so that the employee knows the discussion was more than just blowing off steam.

Meetings are one way in which managers can model the behavior they want to see in their department. Employees watch the way managers treat them and others. They notice whom you acknowledge and how you acknowledge them. They watch how new ideas are accepted or cut off, and whether the established feedback loop is functional or merely an exercise in lip service.

THE SILENT TREATMENT

Sometimes people come to meetings and simply sit. Even when you question them directly, they offer only perfunctory responses. What lies behind such behavior? Often, it's the perception that this is yet another useless meeting in which input and opinions don't really matter. Is it? This is a good opportunity to evaluate the reasons for meetings in your work group, the structure of the agendas, and the conduct of the meetings. Perhaps the meetings are important only to you, or it's your higher-ups who mandate the meetings. Are there more efficient ways for you to convey or collect information? Employees who have heavy workloads (and who doesn't?) may resent meetings that take them from their assigned tasks, especially when there are no mechanisms for them to make up the lost time.

KEEP A SENSE OF HUMOR

Humor is a great way to defuse situations before they become volatile or frustrating. However, it's important to know the difference between finding humor, which is appropriate and often useful, and cracking jokes, which is nearly always inappropriate. Humor arises from situations and carries the unspoken message of shared perspectives; it allows people to have fun. Jokes often poke fun at situations or people.

MASTERING MEETINGS

Setting the Agenda

Ask people how they feel about meetings and in most cases there is a negative reaction, usually because people feel that meetings accomplish very little.

Someone once defined a committee as a group of the unwilling, picked from the unfit, to do the unnecessary. Some meetings can seem just like that, but they don't have to be. By using a few fairly simple guidelines, meetings can be productive and—dare we say it—(almost) fun.

ORGANIZING MEETINGS AND OBTAINING RESULTS

Meetings are an exchange of ideas, information, or opinions by a group of people who play an active role to achieve specific results. This is in contrast to conferences in which most of the audience is in a passive mode, listening to a series of speakers. Unlike most meetings, which only have a few people, conferences can have dozens if not hundreds of participants.

The most frequent criticism of meetings is that "they don't achieve much."

People are quite prepared to put effort into a meeting if they can see a result. But it is extremely frustrating to do your homework, then find that there is no real outcome. "We only talked. Nothing was decided!" If this happens, it's not too surprising that the reaction to the next invitation is: "Not another meeting—what a waste of time!"

ARE MEETINGS NECESSARY?

Some managers automatically seem to call meetings if there is anything to discuss, without ever appearing to consider whether a meeting is the best way to communicate.

Have you ever been in a meeting where a significant portion of it was a conversation between the chairperson and one or two other participants? Quite frequently the others are wondering why they have to sit there for twenty minutes listening to something that is irrelevant (to them) and that could have been handled via e-mail, a telephone call, or a smaller meeting.

Other people call a meeting to impart information that could easily be e-mailed or otherwise distributed in written form. A good example of this would be the announcement of a revised but straightforward procedure. If no discussion or clarification of the procedure is necessary, why call a meeting?

Decide what your objectives are, and determine the best method of achieving each one.

FOCUS ON RESULTS,
RATHER THAN SUBJECTS

An agenda for a meeting is intended not only as a checklist for the chairperson, but also to help participants prepare. When an agenda is based on subjects rather than objectives it may read as follows:

- Minutes of the last meeting
- Progress on computer project

- Lunchtime phone cover
- Improving communications
- Any other business

This agenda might very well remind the chairperson of the subjects to be covered and in what order, but if you were to receive that agenda as a participant, could you adequately prepare for the meeting? Unless you knew the background behind each of the headings, probably not.

Participants usually also want a meeting to achieve results, but with this type of agenda they can only guess at the underlying intention.

FOCUS ON RESULTS

When setting an agenda, make sure to include results-oriented objectives. Based on the aforementioned agenda, a revised agenda might look like this:

- Confirm that actions agreed on at the last meeting have been taken.
- Decide actions, individual responsibilities, and deadlines for phase three of the computer project.
- Set up and agree on a workable schedule for lunchtime phone cover in our department.
- Decide how to find out how our customers (internal and external) feel about the service we provide and discuss who should take care of which problem area defined by customers.

This type of agenda may lengthen the meeting, but the outcomes will be worth it, and in the long term it may result in even fewer meetings.

KEEPING MEETINGS SHORT AND TO THE POINT

Do you attend or run meetings that contain "any other business" (AOB) on the agenda? AOB supposedly allows time to cover any additional issues not listed on the agenda: typically the rubbish that nobody can find a slot for. Frequently the same old trivial subjects come up every time. Even when sensible issues are mentioned, the rest of the group has had no notice and therefore often lacks the necessary information to contribute to the discussion. The next ten minutes is spent deciding that nothing can be decided yet. Not very productive!

CURTAIL TOPIC DRIFT IN BOTH MINUTES AND DISCUSSION

Do the minutes of a meeting you receive a week later sometimes bear little resemblance to what actually transpired?

What typically happens is that the chairperson, who is usually also responsible for note-taking, scribbles furiously while trying to control the meeting. First, it is hard to perform both roles (chairperson and "secretary") simultaneously—one or the other usually suffers. To take a cynical view, some chairpersons, if unsure, write down what they wanted to hear anyway. Second, you and the other attendees cannot see what is being jotted down, so you don't know whether the notes match or even relate to what was just said. These factors set the stage for errors.

When chairing a meeting, consider asking someone to act as an assistant. They can take notes in several ways: low-tech, by using a flipchart; or on a laptop/tablet that hooks onto a projector. Regardless of how it's done, the information will be visible to everyone. If a mistake occurs, it will be easily spotted and corrected.

You can then issue the notes as "minutes." Often, most people only want to know what was decided, what has to be done, by whom, and by when. Try asking those at the meeting what they want the minutes to contain. Most will say, "Keep it simple!"

Another dilemma occurs when a manager is chairing a meeting and also has to be a leading contributor to one or more agenda items. As a contributor, the need is to input or discuss information whereas, as chairperson, the role is to control the input and ensure that it is relevant to the objective(s).

This dilemma results in a potential conflict of interest, making it easy for you, the manager, to talk too much on your topic or try to manipulate events in your favor. Furthermore, most people who attend meetings are reluctant to try and call the chairperson to order (especially if that person is their boss as well).

Consider using a stand-in to chair the portion of the meeting where you need to act as a leading contributor. It is an excellent development opportunity for someone who is working toward a management position. Also:

1. Discuss the objective(s) with your stand-in before the meeting to ensure she understands what you are trying to achieve.
2. When handing over the chair during the meeting, explain that the stand-in will control the next item(s), and that includes your input.

If you have to be a prominent contributor throughout most of the meeting, you might want to let your stand-in chair the entire meeting.

ENSURE THAT PARTICIPANTS UNDERSTAND THEIR ROLE

Have you ever attended a meeting where you thought the objective was to make a decision, only to find that the decision was to be made by someone else and you were simply being consulted?

For example, at a meeting with an agenda item of new software, the group thought they were going to be asked to discuss requirements and decide what new software would be of benefit to the department. Before the meeting they talked about possible useful additions. As the meeting progressed, however, it became clear that the manager only wanted to consult them about their ideas so that she could decide on the final list of software, also taking into account the needs of a second section reporting to her. The group saw their role as "decision-making," but the manager saw their role as "providing information." This point was not clarified until thirty minutes into the agenda item, and as a result time and energy was wasted.

GET A COMMITMENT TO ACT

Consider the following example. The meeting went well, and everyone seemed comfortable with the outcome and action plan. At the next meeting, progress was discussed, and Fred suddenly commented:

"Well, I didn't actually agree to do that, you know. You just assumed that I would." To which you reply, "But I'm sure you agreed to it last time."

More accurately, maybe you thought Fred agreed. After all, most people try their best to take the necessary action by the given deadline. There are some people, however, who seem to make a career out of avoiding any responsibility. They succeed in their evasions because no one says specifically: "Fred, will you take responsibility for . . . ?" Sometimes we assume agreement: If the person says nothing, it is assumed that he or she has accepted the consensus.

So insist upon a "public" agreement by each person to take the relevant action by a specific date. A simple "yes" on their part in front of the group will suffice. Any misunderstanding will then be avoided at that point.

MAKING EFFECTIVE PRESENTATIONS

Imparting Information

Presenting means formally imparting information, opinions, and/or ideas to others so that they are not only heard but also understood. Presenting *proposals* goes one step further by adding the element of persuasion in a formal situation (usually to a group).

As a manager, your ability to effectively impart information to groups is vital. To be an effective manager, you must get across your message and be understood. We have all sat through a poor presentation at some time or another. How much of it did you absorb? Your recommendations will only be accepted—which is the whole point of the exercise—if you are able to present your proposal effectively.

MAKE TIME TO REHEARSE

Almost everyone at some time or other has had to sit through an ill-prepared presentation: unclear objectives, no real structure, poor or inappropriate visual aids, rambling delivery, no sense of what the audience wants, running out of time, blah, blah, blah. Before you know it you've tuned out and are surreptitiously checking your smartphone for texts.

A few years ago, a board of directors instructed ten senior managers to prepare a fifteen-minute presentation outlining budget requirements for the coming financial year. Because of the number of presentations, the managers were told that the fifteen-minute deadline was mandatory. All of the managers except one stuck to this time limit and obtained what they asked for (give or take 10 percent). The manager who tried to overrun was stopped before he even reached his main point. Not surprisingly, he received significantly less budget than the others. He complained bitterly to his boss, saying that his presentation had taken far longer than he had anticipated. His boss asked him if he'd rehearsed and timed his presentation. Exit shame-faced manager stage left!

Therefore, ensure that you do at least one run-through . . . to your partner, a colleague, to the mirror if necessary—any "audience" will suffice. Even with good preparation, the actual delivery usually takes longer (sometimes shorter) than expected. The trial run should reveal most problems and allow you to rectify them and help reduce any natural nervousness.

Also remember to have "Plan B," an available summary slide or PowerPoint showing just the main points of your proposal in case you find yourself running short on time.

GAIN THEIR INTEREST EARLY

Who hasn't suffered through a presentation, wondering "What is this really about?" or "Why do I need to listen to this?" and of course "When is it going to be over?"

For example, a person from a finance department spent over an hour explaining last year's results and next year's budget to a group of managers—lots of detail and "accountant-speak." After the presentation, most of the managers saw it as a waste of time. The few who had managed to "tune in" throughout the whole hour went off delighted with the prospect of having some extra cash in their budgets next year to buy desperately needed capital equipment. The others only found out later, as the requests from these attentive managers went in ("So that's what it was all about!").

If the accountant had emphasized the extra cash early on, she would have had a far more attentive audience throughout the entire presentation. But she failed to gain their interest. Many of them missed the salient point—that there was money to be spent.

So if you want people to listen, grab their attention early. The best way of doing this is to offer a benefit. Suppose the accountant had cut to the chase and said, "I am delighted to tell you that there is $X available next year for new capital equipment, which we know you all desperately need. Before I talk about next year's budget, let's go over how everyone generated the cash this year so that we can do more of the same, hopefully with a similar effect." If you were one of those managers in the audience, would you now be listening?

BE YOURSELF

There are good public speakers, and then there are the rest of us (well most of the rest of us, anyway). It's easy to admire an effective presenter and think: "I wish I could copy her style. Clear, confident, persuasive— I'm so jealous!" While there is nothing wrong in learning from skilled or polished presenters, difficulties occur when imitation is taken too far.

For example, during a presentation skills course, one participant gave an impression of a demented puppet, hopping around, waving his arms, and jerking his body back and forth. At first the class thought it was nerves, but later he explained that his boss had told him he was too boring and to put some life into his speech. So the man took the suggestion to heart, imitating his sales manager boss, whose style of public speaking was rather like a fire-and-brimstone preacher in the Old West. Although that style may have worked for the boss, in this individual it looked downright strange, and it distracted from the points he was trying to make.

Although it's fine to learn from others, do not copy them. Develop your own style and, above all, be yourself! Try to capitalize on your strengths. If you're an introvert who usually talks quietly, occasionally speak louder to make a point—people will really listen. The opposite is true for boisterous personalities—if they say something more softly, it usually gets attention and has a dramatic effect (reserve such techniques for your most important points).

Analyze your weaknesses, and work out how to correct and counter them in such a way that you are comfortable. Remember we're much more aware of our own flaws than others are. Most people are so caught up in their own lives they likely won't notice quirks and mistakes unless we call attention to them.

Gimme a Break!

Have you ever sat through a nonstop presentation that lasted an hour or more? By the end, nature is likely calling very loudly (perhaps screaming), and rigor mortis has started in the gluteus maximus and elsewhere along the back and legs. Aside from that, you probably didn't absorb much of what was said. Most people's span of concentration seems to be around twenty minutes. After that, their attention usually deteriorates rapidly.

Once the presentation skills course participant relaxed and eliminated the unnatural theatrics, his presentations became far more spontaneous and interesting.

PICTURES ARE MEMORABLE

So many presentations seem to consist of purely verbal information or, if visual aids are used, copies of very complex charts or tables. Although PowerPoint and similar software such as Apple Keynote, Adobe Persuasion, and Flowboard have improved the readability of information, there's still a problem with too much verbal data. You need to pare it down to the few essential points, or better yet, use a picture.

If you are trying to make a point, which method do you think will have more impact: plowing through a detailed verbal or written explanation of a new sign or a picture of the new sign itself? Most people remember pictures better than words, provided that the picture is relevant. Showing someone a picture of a new piece of large equipment will be more memorable than simply talking about it.

The same applies to easy-to-understand graphs. For example, a simple pie chart of costs versus income not only illustrates the main point but is easily remembered by the audience. If you want to provide detailed breakdowns, you can create takeaways or handouts in an easy-to-read format.

REMEMBER THE THREE TS

A basic failing in too many presentations is that the audience has no idea what to expect. They are never told why the presentation is being given, what will be covered, or how long it will take. In short, they are left in the dark.

The presenter may know where she is going, but it doesn't occur to her to let the audience in on the secret. Some very brave soul might venture, "What is the point of this?" but that sort of interjection is extremely rare. The audience is far more likely to sit tight and hope that the purpose will eventually become clear. When it does, the audience members then have to think back over the previous ten or twenty minutes to try and remember the essential information.

When you're trying to impart information or persuade, the audience must understand the objective and the relevance of what you are saying early on. Sometimes later is too late—the presenter has already lost the audience and/or they've missed out on essential points!

An easy way to avoid this is to use the "three Ts": **Tell** them what you are **going** to tell them, then **actually tell** them, then **tell** them what you **have told** them.

You can apply this method to all your presentations—possibly with one or two slight additions—as follows:

1. Tell them what you are going to tell them (the objective, why you are talking to them, how you will get there and how long they will have to listen).
2. Tell them (use a logical structure and keep to the point).
3. Tell them what you have told them (in summary form containing: first, essential information to remember; and second, your proposal and its chief benefits).

FOLLOW UP AND FOLLOW THROUGH

Most meetings end with the need for further attention to key agenda items. Even when you've assigned these responsibilities during the meeting, you need to follow up to make sure employees have the resources and information they need. Do you need to pave the way for interaction with another department? Do employees need your help to access information or data? Your follow-through is essential.

Follow-through after a meeting tends to be more effective when a summary of its intentions appears in writing. In other words, send a memo! If the meeting involved a large number of people or an entire department, post a printed copy of the follow-through memo where people will see it—above the copy machine, in the break room, by the doorway. Enterprising managers even post important information in the restrooms. The memo should clearly but briefly state the following:

- The problem
- The agreed-upon or determined solution
- The tasks involved in implementing the solution
- Who is responsible for each task
- The timeline for completing the tasks
- The method for measuring the solution's success

Often there is no reason for a follow-up meeting unless the solution failed to perform as expected. Even so, people like to know what happened as a result of their discussion and input. Make sure to communicate the outcomes of implemented changes and solutions, either as cursory agenda items on subsequent meetings or through memos or e-mails. Solicit employee feedback no matter what your formal assessment method; sometimes an apparent success resurfaces as another issue. Most important, thank people for their suggestions and participation.

PERFORMANCE AND EVALUATION

Meeting Expectations

It seems that there should be a clear and definable relationship between performance and evaluation. You should be able to measure, precisely and objectively, whether the employee does the right things in the right ways. The problem is, performance is not precise and objective. Human interactions are subjective; they involve factors of judgment and perception that exceed the capability of precise, objective measures.

Say, for example, that an employee's job is to make six widgets in an hour. Counting to six is easy enough, but there's more to measuring performance than counting. It's also necessary to determine if the widgets are made correctly. Is there a standard of deviation that's acceptable? If so, is it a precise measurement (each widget can be no more than 0.0032 of an inch larger or smaller than the template) or is it a judgment (each widget feels smooth to the touch)? Must the employee complete one widget every ten minutes, or is it okay for the employee to make all six in the last fifteen minutes of each hour? Can the employee make twelve widgets in one hour, then none in the next hour?

Performance Evaluation Structures

Performance evaluation structures range from the nearly nonexistent (a few comments scribbled on the back of a telephone message note) to the compulsive (the minutiae of a job's tasks itemized and delineated on multiple-page documents). Some take their structures because they must (such as reviews mandated by government or licensing entities), and others because managers and employees alike inherently dislike evaluating performance.

Now suppose it's another employee's job to sell six widgets an hour. Is the standard simply sales, or does it factor in returns? What if there are problems with the phone lines, or the employee calls forty prospective customers but can't convince any of them to actually buy a widget? These are variables beyond the employee's control, yet they directly affect the employee's ability to perform.

In reality, objectivity is difficult. It would be so much easier for everyone if it were possible to devise a universal set of standards. But it's not, and that's a good thing. Many jobs require variability and flexibility. People are different in their needs as well. If there's one lesson you should know by this time in your life, it's that "one size fits all" really doesn't fit anyone.

Company Size Matters

On one end of the continuum are small or family-owned companies that might never formally evaluate anyone's performance. When there are just a few employees, it's pretty obvious when someone's not pulling a full load. There's no place to hide, no way to blend anonymously into a department or work group. Each individual has unique and important responsibilities; failing to meet them puts the company at grave (and usually imminent) risk. People who work in such settings tend to have strong motivations for being there and equally strong commitments to the company and its success. Many of them are likely to be family members. Performance evaluation might mean a pat on the back for an extraordinary success or a dressing down for screwing up.

Large corporations reside at the other end of the continuum. New employees typically receive a written manual that defines the company's expectations on everything from job tasks and responsibilities to shift hours and break periods. The performance evaluation structure is often rigid, commonly a numeric scale of some sort. However, within this apparently confining structure there is room for wide variation in performance. An employee can function at a substandard or mediocre level for a defined period of time without direct consequence to the company.

Live Up to the Contract

Union contracts often define performance standards, measures, and evaluation procedures. In most situations, you cannot change any of these (and often other) elements of the job without a written amendment to the contract. Whether the employee wants or agrees to the change is irrelevant; actions that violate contracts can have serious and far-reaching consequences.

Most companies are somewhere in the middle of these two extremes. As small companies grow, they often add bits and pieces of formality to address specific needs that arise—to deal with the first new employee who doesn't work out, or determine how and when to give someone a raise. Despite the need for their existence, performance evaluations can be a major annoyance for managers and employees alike. Even when there are stringent guidelines, not all employees and circumstances fit within them. And when there are minimal or no guidelines, it's difficult to say to an employee, "Your performance needs improvement."

Performance and Pay

Many performance evaluation systems tie an employee's evaluation to his or her salary. Get a good evaluation, get a raise. Get an average or a poor evaluation, and the money stays the same. This establishes incentives (or disincentives) for managers to slant evaluations to meet needs other than performance issues. A manager might give a mediocre employee a better-than-deserved evaluation because the employee needs the raise—often with the hope that the employee will know this and be motivated to do better as a show of gratitude. Such motivation is likely to be short-lived, if it surfaces at all.

An employee whose performance is substandard might not know this and believe the inflated evaluation to be accurate. Since the evaluation is the perception of performance that becomes part of the employee's records, it becomes difficult if not impossible to go back later to coach the employee about performance that really hasn't changed. Conversely, a manager facing a tight budget might decide that no one will receive higher than an average performance evaluation to avoid having to give raises that could push the budget to the brink of layoffs. While the manager might believe this action is justified because it will save everybody's jobs, employees are likely to feel cheated—they've been giving their best, yet the company views their performance as not good enough.

PERFORMANCE EVALUATION STRUCTURES

Reviews That Work

Regardless of its form, a formal evaluation structure benefits managers, employees, and companies. Say your star employee makes a huge mistake that costs the company big money and has your superiors all over your case. It's a major screwup, and everyone in the department knows about it. Will you remember it in six months, when it's time to do that employee's formal performance evaluation? If so, to what level of detail? The reality is that memories quickly fade, even (or perhaps especially) bad ones. You might swear at the time that you'll never forget, but you will. That's why notes to yourself about important incidents—both positive and negative—are a good idea.

And if that's not problematic enough, other employees will remember—but not necessarily the whole or true story. Employees talk, and as they do the details change. (Remember the childhood game of telephone?) It's not that people intentionally misrepresent the facts. They might have had limited knowledge in the first place, just a piece of the whole picture. So they fill it in, because everybody likes stories with details and endings. And memories fade—even theirs. What people can't quite remember, they create. It's human nature.

MANY SHAPES AND STYLES

There are any number of approaches, methods, and systems for evaluating job performance. If your company doesn't have one yet, you can go online to find resources to learn more about various performance evaluation systems. The particular structure your company uses isn't nearly as important as the fact that it has a structure of some sort in place.

Communicate! Communicate!

Regular communication—daily or at least weekly—is the most effective way to both monitor and shape employee performance. It remains your most effective tool as a manager. Don't save things, good or bad, for a formal evaluation meeting. Nothing you or the employee says in a formal meeting should come as a surprise to either one of you.

A well-designed performance evaluation system includes processes to document extraordinary experiences at the time that they happen (and ideally to address them with involved employees at the time they occur). The most traditional structure features an annual review, usually on the anniversary of the employee's hire date, with supplemental quarterly meetings. Some companies review salary and performance at the same time, while others separate them. Be sure you know your company's policies; your mistakes could cost employees money.

STRUCTURE MEANS CONSISTENCY

Most of the time, you're better off following the structure your company uses, consistently and without deviation. This prevents, or at least minimizes, the likelihood that the evaluation will return to haunt you. And most managers don't like playing the bad guy. A performance evaluation system provides the documented support that you need to present your perspective or defend your position. From morale to legalities, a formal performance evaluation structure truly does benefit and protect everyone.

Some managers hate paperwork, but this doesn't make it okay to avoid structured procedures, like performance reviews. Consider Beverly's situation.

It didn't matter why the paperwork was necessary; Beverly just hated it and avoided dealing with it at just about all costs. Her employees generally admired this attitude; it positioned her as somewhat of a rebel, making her seem to belong more to them than to upper administration. Clarence was one of those employees. In the two years he reported to Beverly, he hadn't had a single performance evaluation. He didn't work any less hard as a result; in fact, he put a lot of time and effort into his work because it felt less bureaucratic than the typical corporate environment. Of course, Clarence didn't get a raise during this time, either, since the company linked raises to performance. But he didn't really mind; he was well paid already, and he believed all it would take was a good word from Beverly and he could circumvent that part of the process, too.

Before he got around to asking Beverly to do that, the company adopted new policies and procedures that forced Beverly to do formal performance evaluations for all of her employees. To his surprise, Clarence discovered that Beverly wasn't entirely happy with his performance. She perceived issues in several key areas of his job responsibilities and asked him to propose an improvement plan. Because of his relatively low measures on the formal evaluation, Clarence received a mediocre raise. He felt betrayed and stabbed in the back. Yes, he could see that he had tripped himself up in certain things, but that wasn't really his fault since no one (such as Beverly) had told him he was on the wrong track. Clarence filed a grievance.

PRESENT THE
PERFORMANCE EVALUATION

For many managers, evaluating an employee's performance is not nearly as difficult as sharing that evaluation with the person. No matter how objective you are, there are emotions attached. People like to hear good things about themselves, and sometimes hearing about the need to improve sounds like criticism. The way you present your comments goes a long way toward shaping the employee's perceptions of his or her performance as well as feelings about what you say.

"Corporate culture matters. How management chooses to treat its people impacts everything—for better or for worse."

—Simon Sinek, business consultant

Schedule your performance evaluation meeting so you have plenty of time to address questions and concerns that arise. Establish ground rules at the start of the meeting. "I will tell you my assessment of your performance for each measure, then give you an opportunity to share your perspectives and comments. I ask that you not interrupt me, and I promise I won't interrupt you."

Stay focused on the topics at hand and keep digressions to a minimum. Give examples of observable behavior to support your comments. If issues surface that need further discussion, schedule another appointment to address them. Take notes, and encourage the employee to do the same. Offer the employee the opportunity to add his or her comments (on a separate page) to the evaluation packet that becomes part of the employee's file.

Present improvements from a positive perspective as much as possible. "You've done a great job developing a system for monitoring report status. Let's take a look at some ways that you can streamline your workflow to be more efficient." If there is bad news, it shouldn't be news to the employee. He or she should know, or at least suspect, that there is a problem. Be direct in presenting the problem, and have a sense of what action you intend to take in response. Conclude the meeting with a plan for improvement, whether this means correcting performance deficiencies or helping the person take steps toward his or her career goals.

IDENTIFY PERFORMANCE ISSUES

Focus on Behavior

A performance appraisal should incorporate the employee's areas of accomplishment as well as identify areas for improvement. Again, nothing you say in a performance appraisal meeting should come as a surprise to the employee—good or not so good. As manager, you should have ongoing interactions with employees that keep you and them aware of any performance deficiencies.

While you want to keep things friendly, this is not a casual chat. It could be the first step to the end of a job for this employee, although you hope it's the beginning of the turnaround you need to see. Meet someplace that assures privacy. Your office is fine if it has floor-to-ceiling walls and a door that closes. Otherwise, meet in a conference room or arrange to use someone else's office.

Find the Right Balance

The tendency in performance evaluations is for managers to focus on what improvements an employee needs to make. This is of course essential. But it is also important to acknowledge the employee's talents and contributions and to recognize growth and development that has already taken place.

Come to a performance evaluation with a clear written agenda of what you want to cover. Have documentation of the problems you want to discuss—notes, memos, copies of e-mails, work that had to be redone, or whatever other evidence is relevant. Be discreet, of course—have the items in a file folder, not spread out on the desk when the employee arrives. Lastly, know, at least in general, what you want the employee to do to remedy the situation.

FOCUS ON SPECIFIC AND OBSERVABLE BEHAVIORS

If you or someone else didn't observe an event, it didn't happen and you can't really talk about it. This is not a meeting about feelings or suspicions. It is about tangible actions and behaviors—work that didn't get done, assignments done incorrectly, inappropriate e-mail messages, and so on—that are creating performance problems for this employee. Provide the employee with actual examples. You might say:

- "Here is the memo you sent to accounts receivable about the Robinson account. It has the wrong balances, and you erroneously flagged the account as past due."
- "I've gotten complaints from other departments about the number of jokes you forward by e-mail. Here are copies of messages that people have given me."
- "When we established the timeline for the widgets, you agreed that it was reasonable and would accommodate the kinds of delays that might arise. I've checked with you every week, and you've said you had everything under control. The widget prototype still isn't to manufacturing, though the timeline says it should have been in full production six weeks ago."

What do you do when the problem is vague, such as a bad attitude? You might see the crux of the problem as attitude, and that could indeed be the case. But you still need tangible evidence—and usually there's an abundance of it, such as yelling at coworkers, badmouthing others, showing up late, and leaving early. Again, be specific and provide examples.

Unless you've asked other employees if you can use their names when talking to the problem employee, don't name them. Keep the conversation focused on the employee who is in the room with you and on behaviors rather than personalities. Explain why the behaviors are problems, just to be sure you and the employee have the same understanding (which is not to imply that you must agree).

LISTEN TO THE EMPLOYEE'S PERSPECTIVE

Many employees are surprised when their managers confront them about their performance. Even when you've maintained clear and open communication, the employee might not perceive the situation as serious or as a problem. Before you dismiss the employee's explanations as worthless excuses, you owe it to the person to hear his or her perspective. Listen to the employee's side without interrupting. If you take notes, do so unobtrusively. Listen without judgment and without challenging the employee's perceptions. If you have questions, ask them after the employee has finished speaking.

Sometimes there are issues within a work group or department that at least partially impede the employee's ability to perform necessary job tasks. Antiquated computer equipment, understaffing, inefficient procedures such as multiple signoffs, and many other factors can be legitimate barriers. Sometimes the employee doesn't know how to do a particular task or step in a procedure and doesn't know who to ask, or is afraid to ask, for help. If such factors are present, it's your responsibility to do what is possible to remedy the situation. If there are barriers you can't remove or minimize, it's not really fair or reasonable to hold the employee accountable. It might be necessary for you to modify your expectations or the employee's job responsibilities.

Look for Individual Solutions

If an employee is worth keeping, it's worth your time and energy to find solutions that will work for both of you. Consider additional training through classes or workshops, one-on-one tutoring with a more experienced employee, online or video training, job-shadowing—whatever looks to be effective, efficient, and even a little fun.

JOB PERFORMANCE COACHING

Improving Work-Related Behavior

When we speak of coaching in the context of the work environment, we're addressing the process of formally meeting with an employee to discuss performance issues—and documenting that discussion through a letter or memo that goes to the employee and perhaps to his or her personnel file. In many companies, this is a step in the progressive discipline process. This is not counseling in the sense of "let's uncover what's really bothering you so we can make it better." You are not a therapist; you are a manager. You cannot address psychological problems, even if you know enough to see that they are present. Your role is to say to this employee, "There are problems with your performance that we need to discuss." The bottom line is that you want to improve the employee's work-related problems. If that also fixes his or her personal problems, great. But that's not your primary goal.

Sympathy, but from a Distance

If an employee is having problems at home—with a partner, children, elderly parents, or health—you can lend a sympathetic ear, but you can't intrude into these areas. Recommend that the employee seek outside help. If your company offers an EAP (employee assistance program), refer the employee for assistance. If the problem is related to substance abuse, most state employment laws require companies to follow certain procedures for testing, mandatory counseling, and return-to-work agreements. Be sure to follow your company's policies and procedures.

Often this approach feels cold-hearted and harsh. You are a compassionate human being who genuinely cares about this employee as a person, not just as a productive work unit. And while you can try to focus on the behaviors that you want the employee to change (as you should), you might believe that permanent change will come only when you uncover and somehow address the underlying issues. But that's not your role. Playing therapist (or even friend) can land you and your company in legal hot water. It's a delicate balance indeed, and one that can tip out of control before you know it.

If the employee identifies factors within the workplace that interfere with completing job tasks, establish a plan for you to address those concerns and a time by which you'll get back to the employee with answers or solutions. Every employee has unique needs when it comes to improving job performance, just as each has a unique work style. It's important to establish that this is a serious matter and that you are establishing the framework for remedying the situation. You should also allow the employee to participate at a comfortable level. When the coaching meeting ends, you both should be able to leave with your dignity and self-confidence intact. After all, the employee really has more of a vested interest in improving than anyone else.

DOCUMENTATION IS YOUR FRIEND

It's fine for you to take notes during your meeting—invite the employee to do so as well. Whether you do or not, take another ten or fifteen minutes immediately following the meeting (after the employee leaves) to write down a brief accounting of what transpired. Be sure to do the following:

- Note what specific examples you used, and how the employee responded.
- Write down the details of the improvement plan you agreed upon, as well as the steps that will be necessary to monitor progress.
- Record any contributing factors from the work environment that the employee feels interfere with productivity, as well as your intentions for addressing issues that involve the employee.

Before you commit your thoughts to writing, consider how your words might sound a few months or years from now, coming from a lawyer's mouth. Be sure your comments are factual and maintain the same tangible focus as your meeting. Laws vary among states, but in many the courts can subpoena any written materials you keep—including notes intended only for your use. If you have any doubts or concerns about what constitutes appropriate documentation, check with your company's HR or legal department. Even if your company has a human resources department that handles the legal end of employment, it doesn't hurt for you to know the basics. As a front-line manager, your accountability may be limited when it comes to such matters. As you progress upward in the management hierarchy, however, you must learn more of the details. This is especially true in small companies, as midlevel managers may conduct all human resources functions.

Documentation Is the Best Safeguard

Many managers are leery of committing adverse performance reports to writing, for fear that what they say will come back to bite them in court. However, attorneys who specialize in employment law generally believe documentation is a company's best safeguard against frivolous lawsuits. Written job descriptions and performance appraisals establish procedural consistency. The paper trail that is likely to cause trouble is the one built solely for the purpose of carrying out a particular action. Documentation should support decisions, not create them.

Documentation is a good habit to develop. A good paper trail can demonstrate your and your company's consistency in addressing performance issues and can provide irrefutable evidence of your efforts to help the employee change and improve. More often than not, solid documentation deters rather than encourages lawsuits—especially when both manager and employee sign dated copies. This helps protect you and your company against accusations of wrong-doing down the road, when memories have become selective and faded (on all sides). Depending on your company, this could be more than sage advice—it could be corporate policy. Most companies have written guidelines and procedures for managers to follow.

AGREE TO AN IMPROVEMENT PLAN

After you've shared your concerns and listened to the employee's perspective, it's time to move into action mode. Identifying the problems is the first half of your task; identifying solutions is the second. Although you want the employee to participate in developing an improvement plan, you also want to be sure that plan achieves the goals that are important to you and to the company. Every improvement plan should include three core elements:

- **Specific goals for, and descriptions of, the improvements you want to see.** "Memos that leave this department must be free from grammatical and spelling mistakes."

- **Specific steps for achieving the described improvements.** "I want you to run the spellchecker just before you save or print any document. For the next two weeks, I want to sit down with you at 11 A.M. and 3 P.M. to review all outgoing memos. We will proof them together."
- **Specific methods for measuring performance and assessing improvement.** "I ran the spellchecker on these memos that I showed you, and each had at least seven errors. By the end of one week, I want the memos we review together to have fewer than three errors each. At the end of two weeks, I want every memo we review together to have no errors that the spellchecker is capable of detecting. We'll meet again at the end of two weeks to discuss your improvement."

Depending on the kinds of problems that exist and how complex the employee's job duties are, your improvement plan might consist of a few bulleted items or several pages of expectations and directives. Most improvement plans work best when they include an agreement to meet at determined intervals to review progress and make appropriate revisions. If an employee's problems involve numerous job functions, you might want to develop an incremental plan that attacks one problem at a time. Whatever form the plan takes, put it in writing. At the end, put a sentence that says, "I understand the requested improvements and agree to follow this plan to make them happen" (or words to this effect). Then sign your name and write the date, and have the employee sign. Each of you gets a copy.

TIMELY FOLLOW-UP

In concept, performance is ever-evolving as the employee's skills and knowledge grow and expand. Every employee's performance has room for improvement. Although your company might have formal evaluation meetings just once or twice a year, change (whether to correct a problem or foster growth) requires regular follow-up and monitoring. You should establish the shape and form of this follow-up during the evaluation meeting or at a subsequent meeting if that's how you set things up. What are the employee's obligations and commitments? What are yours? Is the employee going to work with you to establish priorities, present you with realigned priorities, or rely on you to present priorities? Be sure the improvement plan establishes the following:

- A schedule of regular meetings to assess the employee's progress toward improvement
- Suggested improvement actions (expressed in terms of observable behaviors)
- Clear expectations for what each follow-up meeting will cover, and what the employee needs to bring or provide
- Exactly what improvements you expect to see (expressed in terms of observable behaviors), and when you will be satisfied that the desired improvements have taken place
- Consequences for failing to improve

If the employee raised concerns during the evaluation meeting that require your action, give the employee a timeline and sense of structure for expecting responses from you. As the manager, you are responsible for making sure that follow-up occurs, both in terms of the desired behavior changes as well as the meetings or discussions to monitor or confirm the changes. If you don't care enough to follow up, why should the employee care enough to follow through?

MANAGING FORMER COWORKERS

The People You Know

It's exciting to receive a promotion to manager. You're proud of yourself and your accomplishments, and rightly so—you've worked hard to earn your rung on the corporate ladder. Naturally, you can't wait to share your excitement with your coworker friends. They're likely proud of you, too. After all, your promotion is real-life proof that they, too, have a shot at moving up the ladder. You represent possibilities and potential. But they are not your coworkers anymore. And whether they remain your friends depends on numerous variables including whether you've moved up and out or just up, meaning that your former coworkers now report to you.

Promote Fairly

When an organization's promotion policies are clear and everyone follows those policies consistently, people generally perceive promotions as being fair. Those who competed with you for the promotion may be disappointed because they didn't get it, but they will likely be supportive of you in your new role.

It's Monday morning, your first day as manager. You've worked for several years with all the people milling about in the coffee room. But now they return your cheery greeting with cautious reserve. They're not your coworkers anymore. You've moved up, and the ranks have closed behind you. Your former coworkers now report to you and they can't wait to put you to the test. Not in a malicious way, of course—at least not most of them. But they now look to you for answers and action on everything from settling into the day's work routine to customer crises and scheduling snafus. From daily duties to performance ratings and job security, you hold their futures in your hands. They know it more than you do!

Respect Rank and Structure

The U.S. military has long prohibited fraternization across rank, such as between officers and enlisted personnel. Though interaction and even closeness among unit members are essential for top performance, the military perspective is that familiarity undermines authority and the performance of duties. The military expects—and demands—that all personnel respect rank, the military management structure.

USE WHAT YOU KNOW

Getting promoted within your work group might present you with the greatest challenge you will face as a manager. Your key advantage is that you already know these people. You know what they like and don't like about the workplace and about the management styles that direct and regulate the work they do. You know what *you* like and don't like. You may even know what changes the employees in your department desire or expect from a manager. You can use this knowledge to start off on the right foot in your new role. The four Rs can help you move from employee to manager within your work group:

- **Resist** the temptation to make immediate and dramatic changes. Unless changing things is your mandate from upper management, stay the course until you get a feel for what it's like to walk the other side of the line. You need time to allow your new role to broaden and clarify your viewpoint.

- **Review** existing procedures and practices. Meet with employees one-on-one or in small groups to ask them what they think works, doesn't work, and why. Ask what changes they would like to see, and keep the focus on the work. Take notes.
- **Revise** one step at a time. Sometimes one small change makes a very big difference. Use a planned approach that includes some sort of measurement system. Incorporate suggestions from employees to the extent possible, even if only parts and pieces of what they've told you they want.
- **Recognize** the contributions of your employees. Always share and spread the credit. All work tasks require some level of collaboration, cooperation, and synergy—teamwork. Upper-level management knows a good team happens only when there is a good team leader.

The transition from peer to superior is seldom smooth. Your former colleagues, now your subordinates, feel resentment toward you when you give them job assignments and evaluate their job performance. They may react in one or more of these ways:

- Passive-aggressive behavior, in which they seem to be going along with what you say but in reality are undermining your efforts. Passive-aggressive behavior may take the form of doing only and exactly what you tell them to do, not telling you when problems arise or when they know a particular approach won't work.
- Frank anger, in which unhappy former coworkers may be confrontational or give you the "cold shoulder" or silent treatment.

- Sabotage, in which one or more employees may intentionally interfere with work flow such as by "losing" files or phone messages.
- Insubordination and refusal to do work.

These behaviors may be subtle or outright, and there is no single best way to handle them. The most effective approach is to talk with each offender individually. You can work out most grievances by giving people the opportunity to say what's on their minds. It is important to do this in private; nothing fuels disgruntlement like an audience. Hear the person out before you begin speaking. Remember, most of what you hear comes from an emotional base. Say what is necessary to keep the meeting focused on work, but let the person have his or her say.

Be Prompt with Discipline

Do not slack on disciplinary matters! When an employee puts you to the test by violating company policy, ethical standards, or even laws, you *must* take prompt and appropriate action. Failing to do so at the very least diminishes your authority within your work group and at worst may make you complicit in the violation.

When it's your turn to talk, acknowledge the person's feelings and then move the conversation to work. Use a collaborative tone. Do not apologize for your promotion; you have no reason to feel bad about it. "I know you had hoped to receive this promotion, Frank. You've been here a long time and you have a lot of good ideas. I have some ideas, too, and over the next few months I look forward to meeting with you and the others to discuss our department's procedures and direction."

When the behavior is a serious offense—violates company policy, jeopardizes customer relationships, or puts people at risk—you have no choice but to invoke your company's disciplinary policies. Because you are a new manager, you will want to involve at least your boss and probably a representative from your human resources department. Your company may stipulate other processes, depending on the contracts and working relationships (such as unions) that may exist.

ANGRY EMPLOYEES, ANGRY MANAGERS

Finding the Underlying Issues

Anger is common in the workplace. People get upset with other people, circumstances, and situations. We get angry when we feel afraid, sad, threatened, insecure, disappointed—when things are out of our control. Anger elicits a response when other efforts fail to do so, which can give a false sense of control. Anger is uncomfortable for others to experience, so they often do whatever it takes to put an end to their discomfort—which often means placating the angry person by giving what the person wants.

When Is Anger More Than Blowing Off Steam?

Anger becomes dangerous when others feel threatened by the person's expression of it. Such expressions may include direct or indirect threats, yelling, and actions such as slamming or throwing things, and physical gestures or contact.

THE STRAW THAT BREAKS THE CAMEL'S BACK

Everyone gets angry, and everyone has gotten angry with the wrong people for the wrong reasons at the wrong times. For most people, the expression of anger represents the culmination of feelings they can no longer control. However, the actual event that sends them over the edge is often something minor that might not even be related to the reasons they're angry. The challenge for you as the manager is to identify and expose the underlying issues. Here's an example.

Carolyn, an administrative assistant in the accounting department, blew up when Stephen, an accounts payable clerk, stopped at her desk to tell her the break room was out of coffee. "I've had it! Get your own damn coffee!" she screamed at him. "I'm not the only one in this department who can walk two lousy blocks to the store to buy a package of fine grind! It doesn't take a college degree! Just go get it yourself!"

John, the department manager, heard Carolyn shouting and came out of his office to see what was going on. He asked her to take a walk with him. Once they were outside the building, he asked her what had happened. Still agitated, Carolyn repeated her exasperation that everyone in the department seemed to believe buying coffee was her responsibility and hers alone. "I don't even drink coffee!" she said. "Nowhere in my job description does it say that it's my job to buy the coffee! No one notices anything else I do, but when we run out of coffee, everyone comes running to me!"

John immediately agreed that it was not Carolyn's job to buy coffee. It wasn't even a job responsibility at all, for anyone. It was a pattern the department slipped into because she had once been willing to do it, he observed, but it certainly wasn't an aspect of her job. John assured Carolyn that he would post a memo asking the coffee drinkers to decide among themselves how to maintain the coffee supply.

As they walked and talked, it became clear to John that Carolyn was very frustrated because her job was not giving her the opportunities to advance that she had anticipated it would when she took the job three years ago. In her career plan, she was to have been an accounting clerk by this time—but here she was, still an admin assistant running to the store to buy coffee. "I know just as much as the other clerks, probably more, but no one notices that I'm the one who corrects their statements and records," Carolyn told John. "There have been three openings in receivables in the past six months, but you've selected someone else each time."

John explained that the department used educational requirements to screen applicants, and that Carolyn didn't have an undergraduate degree with a major in any of the required fields. He agreed that she did have exemplary knowledge of the department and its functions, and said he would check with HR to see if there was a way to flex the education requirements to accommodate Carolyn's degree in communications. John also reminded Carolyn that he had an open-door policy because he wanted people to come to him with their concerns. If she had come to talk to him when the job openings were first posted, he could have talked to HR then. As it was, there weren't any vacancies now, and he didn't know when one would surface. John and Carolyn agreed to meet in one week to discuss what John was able to find out from HR.

Carolyn felt unappreciated and unfairly overlooked when it came to promotional opportunities. This aroused nagging doubts about whether she truly was qualified for the job she wanted to have; if no one noticed how good she was, maybe she wasn't really that good. So she tried even harder to get John and others in her department to notice her work and recognize her abilities— she left Post-it notes on people's desks whenever she corrected paperwork they submitted that was incomplete, and joined in on discussions about department procedures and accounting matters. That no one picked up on these attempts to gain recognition further fueled both her frustration and her self-doubt.

Assuaging the Situation

As Carolyn's manager, John should have had a better understanding of Carolyn's career goals. Career planning was a key part of the company's performance standards and evaluation process. Each employee met with his or her manager every six months to review progress toward stated goals and objectives. If Carolyn was vague in these meetings, John should have pinned her down at least to be assured that he understood what she hoped to accomplish during her employment and in her career. When Carolyn hit crisis mode, however, John reacted swiftly and appropriately:

- He removed Carolyn from the scene. When someone bursts into a rage in front of other people, it's nearly impossible for him or her to back down without losing face. Since frustration and fear are among the core emotions that ignite anger, a person in outburst mode is not going to willingly validate these emotions by surrendering. Removing an angry person from any audience removes the need for the person to continue raging. It also provides an opportunity for the person to regain composure and dignity.
- He agreed with Carolyn that her feelings were valid. This put them both on the same side, giving them common ground from which to work toward a mutually acceptable solution.
- He stayed focused on the issues. While John didn't support Carolyn's behavior, he didn't criticize it, either. He directed the discussion to tangibles—Carolyn's disappointment and

frustration about not being promoted, and the company policies that impeded her efforts. This allowed John to present possible solutions.

- He concluded the discussion with tangible actions and a follow-up plan. Without making promises he might not be able to keep, John told Carolyn exactly what he would do to try to resolve her frustration and when they would meet for further discussions.

Carolyn's anger of course had nothing to do with poor Stephen, whose words simply happened to be the trigger that released Carolyn's frustrations.

ANGRY MANAGERS

Although angry employees are a key concern for most managers, angry managers are often a key concern for employees. Employees are unfortunately convenient targets when a manager blows a gasket—again, often for reasons completely unrelated to the anger. Managers, like employees, sometimes carry problems from home or other dimensions of their lives into the workplace. A fight with your spouse or kids might start your day with a sour outlook. Because you know you have to go to work and deal with all the pressures there, you try to stay calm and collected at home so you can at least leave with the delusion of peace and harmony. But when you get to work, an employee says or does something that triggers those feelings you've swallowed, and back up they rush. Before you know it, you're dumping all over this employee whose only offense was to be in the wrong place at the wrong time saying the wrong thing.

The Usefulness of EAPs

There are many pressures in today's world, both at home and at work. Your company's employee assistance program (EAP) can be a good resource for employees and managers alike. Most EAPs provide short-term counseling to help people find solutions to their problems. Many EAPs extend consultation services to managers and supervisors, offering advice and recommendations about workplace issues. Such interventions help managers deal with stress and the factors that cause it, and they can head off problems before they become serious.

Managers can get away with a lot of abusive behavior toward employees, or at least they think they can. They can close the door and say what they want and get away with it—for the short term. But the toll in loss of morale and even legal issues at some point catches up. Employees learn quickly to read the moods of their managers. When managers have problems at home or are feeling pressure from other departments or their superiors, employees learn to anticipate venting and tirades. Some duck for cover behind work projects that take them out of the office, while others get angry themselves.

The Misuse of Anger

Sometimes managers use anger as a way of turning employees against the company. A manager may not like the direction of the company, for example, so he incites anger in his employees, hoping that he can hurt the company by hurting them. This gets everybody angry and unites the work group in battle. Although employees are often unaware that this is what's going on, they are likely to suffer the consequences in terms of lost opportunities and bad reputations.

When a manager loses control, and particularly when the loss unleashes anger toward employees, the consequences can be severe and far-reaching. When you feel anger rising within you that you know is going to splash all over some employee, take a deep breath and ask yourself a few questions:

- Is this employee the source of my anger?
- If so, why?
- If not, who or what is?
- Am I really feeling angry, or am I disappointed?
- What, realistically, can the employee or I do to remedy the situation?
- Can I talk with the employee about this without losing my cool?
- What is the worst that can happen if I just walk away from this and address it later?

If you can't talk to the employee without losing your temper, do whatever you need to do to cool off before you say anything to anyone. Then, before you approach the employee, write some notes to yourself that explain the problem as you see it, what adverse consequences occurred as a result, and what solutions you propose. Stick to this "script" in your conversation (even if you need to refer to your notes while you're talking) to help keep yourself calm and focused.

MANAGING YOUR STRESS

There are a lot of reasons for stress in the workplace, and each individual has unique triggers. In general, workplace stress is the result of tiredness and competing demands, whether at work, at home, or both. We all lead busy lives that seldom make it easy for us to take time off from anything.

Most people feel the greatest amount of stress when they're working hard or long hours and feeling that they're not getting anything in return for their efforts and sacrifices. For some people this recognition is in terms of money (that is, they feel they should be paid more), though more often it is actual recognition that they feel is lacking. Money loses much of its charm after a while, but praise for work well done lives in memory for a long, long time.

Stress at Work, Stress at Home

Life beyond the workplace further adds to stress. Office pressure seems to be worse when our home lives are not what they should be. Either life at home is great but we can't really enjoy it, or life at home is not so great so there is no relief from stress even when we leave for the workplace.

Stress is really about balance. A certain level of stress is necessary in life, of course—without it, we don't feel motivated or interested in doing things. But when there is too much of it, we don't feel motivated or interested, either. If life is all work, fasten your seatbelt—a crash is inevitable. So what can you, as a manager, do? In the first place, recognize the symptoms of your own stress, such as these:

- Anxiety and worrying about things you can't change
- Inability to sleep or lack of adequate sleep
- Fatigue and feelings of exhaustion
- Flying off the handle
- Depression and lack of interest in normally pleasant activities

- Feeling sorry for yourself
- Engaging in passive-aggressive behavior

Even if you don't see these indicators when you look in the mirror or listen to yourself when you're talking with employees, know that the people in your work group have learned to read your moods. They might not know what to do with their interpretations, but your employees become less effective because you are less effective.

Avoidance might be a good diversionary tactic, but it doesn't work over the long haul. An environment based on avoidance becomes confusing and frustrating for everyone. Eventually employees lose track of whether this is a stress day for you, or if the storm has blown over. Either way, they will not be sure how to behave. As the manager, you establish the "stress protocol" for your department and your employees. Others do what you do. If this protocol is not the one you want everyone to follow, change it. Managers need to set clear examples, and being open—even about stress—is one of them. Here are a few ideas:

- If you're feeling stressed, go into your office, close the door, and take a few slow, deep breaths. If you meditate or do yoga, take ten minutes to indulge in these great stress relievers.
- Tell your employees that you're feeling stressed, and offer a brief explanation. "I didn't get enough sleep last night, and I have to get this report finished by noon." This often makes you and your employees feel better.
- Try not to say things you'll regret or have to apologize for later. The "count to ten" rule comes in handy in times of stress. Ten seconds is not too long to pause before responding to a question or a comment, and the extra time to think can save all involved considerable embarrassment and frustration.

- Remind yourself that this is a temporary situation, and it too will pass.
- If a few days off would help, take them. Your department and the company will survive without you.

You also need to watch your lifestyle and encourage your employees to do the same. If your workload is overwhelming, what will make the situation better? Are you taking too much on? Not delegating? What should you do? What can you do? Stress starts with you, so set a positive example. (You're already setting an example of some sort; now's your opportunity to shape it into the one you *want* to set.) What do you need to do when you are stressed out? Do you need a vacation or a long rest? Is so, take the time and do it. And encourage your employees to do the same.

REPLACING A MANAGER

A Responsibility and Opportunity

What is a "bad" manager? Often, this is a judgment that exists in the eye of the beholder. After all, no one is perfect. But what employees perceive as good or bad in a manager is not necessarily the same as what executive management sees in the situation. There are also different levels of "bad" managing. For example, some managers feel such a need for their employees to like them that they gossip with them, even badmouthing the company or its leaders. While this may seem harmless on the surface, these actions ultimately end up costing managers from both sides. Employees soon begin to wonder what their managers say about them, and executives no longer trust gossiping managers to uphold the company's interests.

Now, gossiping is bad, but there are worse things. Consider the scenario in the following section. Although the names have been altered to protect those who wish to remain unidentified, the circumstances are real.

A TRULY TERRIBLE PREDECESSOR

Sometimes the former manager truly can be bad, no matter whose standards form the measurement. Managers can be dictatorial, disorganized, selfish, unfair, lazy, and abusive. Neither employees nor executives appreciate these characteristics (although nearly everyone has had a boss somewhere along the line who has personified them). When you are replacing a manager who was bad by all accounts and standards, you have both a responsibility and an opportunity.

Jonathan joined Wonder Corporation with rave reviews from the upper-level executives who had hired him. Within weeks, however, his employees were singing a very different song. Jonathan seemed to call in sick every time he had accumulated enough leave time to cover a day out of the office. At least once a week he called to say he would be working from home, although no one answered the phone when employees called with questions. When he was in the office, Jonathan was disorganized, volatile, and unpredictable. He flew off the handle for no apparent reason, canceled or missed appointments, redefined assigned projects and tasks without consulting those doing the work, and often refused to make decisions about even the most mundane matters (like ordering toner for the copy machine).

Jonathan played favorites, promoting one person and squelching the ambitions of others. It was never safe to be in Jonathan's good graces because his fancy turned faster than a child's whimsy. Without warning, yesterday's favorite became today's scapegoat. Most of the people Jonathan promoted he soon fired. Jonathan did this to keep the person from showing him up. Ultimately it didn't work because everyone in the office caught on to Jonathan's game. Fortunately, upper management caught on to it as well, and Jonathan was fired. (Upon hearing the news, the employees had a party.)

The new manager, Joanne, started her first day on the job by meeting with everyone. She asked the group to talk about what worked and what didn't, from a process perspective. She explicitly said she did not want to hear names and personal stories. This freed the employees to focus on workflow, assignments, goals, priorities, and other issues related to productivity rather than personality. Over the next two days, Joanne went around to talk privately with each employee, allowing people to express their personal feelings. On Friday of her first week, Joanne called another department meeting. She shared her improvement plan with the group, talking about what seemed to work well and what didn't. She gave everyone a few days to think about and respond to the plan, and then created a revised improvement plan that incorporated many employee suggestions.

Joanne continued talking with employees, both individually and in group meetings. Employees learned they could trust her, and grew to like as well as respect her. Within six months, the department was so far ahead of its goals that it was necessary to revise the plan again.

Cleaning Up Someone Else's Mess

Cleaning up after a bad manager is among the most difficult challenges you can face in your new role. Unless you handle the situation just right, you, too, will look incompetent. All managers, good and bad, have loyal followers. Always assume this to be true. It isn't necessary to treat these employees any differently (and in fact it is probably better for you not to), but it is vital for you to know who they are, because your first mission is to get everybody on board, and the loyalists will be the most resistant. Here are the basic steps to follow:

- Express clear and concise goals and objectives. Explain why these are important to each employee, to the department, and to the company.
- Ask each employee for comments and thoughts. Respond to negative expressions without judgment or attempting to refute them. "Yes, that's an interesting point. We'll come back to that."
- Respond directly but nonconfrontationally to efforts to undermine your authority and the process. If an employee persists,

quietly and calmly request that he or she meet with you in your office after the meeting to discuss those concerns.

- Continue to gather input and information from every employee. Meet with individuals and small work groups as well as the entire department.
- Listen to what people are saying, and also to what they're not saying. Question, nonconfrontationally, what doesn't make sense to you or seems out of context.
- Integrate employee suggestions into improvement plans. If you can't use a suggestion directly, use it indirectly and credit the employee or employees with providing the impetus for the necessary change.
- Be consistent. If you change direction, have a good reason and present it to your employees.

It's easy to turn the last manager into a bad guy, regardless of whether that was actually the case. Human nature causes us to want to look as good as we can; sometimes this tendency (rooted in insecurity) leads us astray. You might be tempted to think that by making someone else look bad, you can at least look better—if not downright good. Resist! Although extremes in perception are common during times of transition, eventually the fog clears and balance returns to judgment. When this happens, you're in a much stronger position if your attributes stand on their own merits. On the flip side, turning the last manager into a bad guy can backfire by instead turning him or her into a martyr. It's also human nature to put a halo on the last manager's head. People forget how bad things really were, and they begin to reminisce about the good old times (however few of them there actually were). Before you know it, you become the bad guy.

REPLACING A "GOOD" MANAGER

What happens when the manager before you was almost superhuman? Those are big shoes to fill. Following a great manager can be just as much of a challenge as replacing a bad manager. As always, good communication is essential. Here are some key points to keep in mind:

- Listen to employees so you know what concerns them, and talk with them so they know what concerns you.
- Confront the ghosts head-on. Ask employees what they liked about the previous manager's approach, and what they would change if they were in your shoes.
- Focus on processes, procedures, and policies. Whether or not employees like you, this is the foundation of the workplace.
- Refrain from presenting your views to change the world at the first meeting. Save your perspective for subsequent meetings, when you can temper your comments with understanding that you acquire by listening to employees' concerns and views.
- Do not comment about the previous manager's ways of doing things. Remain neutral and supportive of the company's goals. Whatever role you're playing, you are above all the face of the company.

Just as with bad, good is in the eye of the beholder. Change doesn't inherently mean the end of good; it can mean a different kind of good. Any good manager can (and should) have an open-door policy in which employees feel comfortable seeking him or her out, an open exchange of ideas, and procedures that support the work group's productivity and happiness.

REBUILDING A WORK GROUP

Creating a New Team

Sometimes a manager steps into an existing work group or department that is intact. The employees are seasoned and knowledgeable, and passing the manager's baton is a smooth process. When the previous manager has been fired, however, it is very likely that the new manager must contend with productivity issues. Other employees might have been fired or transferred as well, leaving some positions vacant. If you are a manager in this type of situation, your mission is to rebuild.

If You're Unclear, You'll Lose Trust

It's important to make sure each person understands his or her role and responsibilities, as well as those of the others in the work group or department. And it's essential to clearly articulate and support new goals and procedures. Ambiguity breeds *mis*trust, and that's not what you need to succeed as a manager.

The need to rebuild can arise from several circumstances. Perhaps there is a new market, making it necessary for a company to revamp its product and service lines to meet changing customer demands. In such a setting, your job as manager is to identify the key strengths and abilities that existing employees offer and look for ways to fit them into the new structure. You will need to motivate employees to feel that they are valued contributors in the new order.

Maybe your company has reorganized because of new ownership or to consolidate operations (save money). The employees who remain are likely to be suspicious and reluctant to support (or even appear to support) new corporate mandates. It is fertile ground for resentment, distrust, anger, and fear. But you're not going to let these negatives grow because you see the situation as a great opportunity. Pull out your parent, coach, and cheerleader hats—you need to mobilize these people. But first, allow for some mourning. While the public view of corporate shakeups tends to spotlight the people who lose their jobs, the employees who remain have also experienced trauma. It can be more distressing to be among the survivors than it is to be among those who get a pink slip.

People need time to assimilate and adjust. A good manager acknowledges these feelings, and then helps employees focus on the future and encourages a positive outlook. After all is said and done, however, your key role is still to craft a cohesive and productive work group. This entails communicating both with the group as a whole and with individual employees to do the following:

- Clarify goals
- Identify roles and responsibilities
- Establish procedures for how people work together
- Get acceptance and support from employees

The sooner you define a clear path, the sooner employees can get on with their work. People recover more quickly when there is a plan in place that helps them move forward, toward new responsibilities and broadened abilities. You, their manager, are the one who can—and must—lead them.

RIDING THE WAVES OF CHANGE

The turbulent 1980s gave rise to the use of a phrase from Shakespeare's *The Tempest* to describe the magnitude of the upheaval in the business world: "sea change." The new environment was dramatically different from the old one, as were the new ways. Such upheavals are like volcanic eruptions: They blow existing structures to oblivion and construct new ones, often simultaneously. One minute there's a mountain and the next there's a smoking crater. But seismic catastrophes make for new hills and valleys and rivers and lakes, a ready-made environment that replaces the old one. In the business world, such eruptions take the form of mergers and acquisitions. One day there's a giant conglomerate that dominates the corporate landscape, and the next there's a smattering of small companies scattered all around.

Things change. It's as much a reality of your career as it is of nature. Companies change, people change, needs change. The typical American worker may have as many as seven careers during his or her working life, and three or four times that many jobs—a significant change in the course of a generation. In commerce, as in nature, change results in new and often unexpected growth. Those who thrive are those who can adapt to new needs and demands, and who can respond to challenging or difficult situations with positive attitudes and actions.

Nowhere is this more true—or more significant—than for managers. Not only must you stay current with changes in your field of expertise, you also must remain up-to-date on laws and regulations that affect the workplace, changes in business practices, and advances in technology. Your company may change ownership. Core employees may leave. You cannot influence these events, so you must keep yourself prepared to accommodate them.

PROMOTING AND HIRING

Finding the Right People

Hiring and promoting people are essential functions within any company. Both offer great potential for mutual benefit—when you handle them properly. Mishandled, however, employment and promotion choices can cost your company far more than money. Studies suggest that hiring and promoting from within is more successful than bringing in outsider candidates. Even so, companies are twice as likely to look beyond their current employee population when new jobs become available. Sometimes, of course, going outside is the only way to acquire new talent that your company needs. So how do you find the best people for the job?

THE RIGHT START

The hiring process varies widely. Small companies, particularly family businesses in small towns, may still do business on the basis of a promise and a handshake. Other companies have extensive procedures and paperwork. Though prospective employees often believe there are laws and regulations that govern the hiring process, legal guidelines are broad, and they target big issues like discrimination and equal opportunity. There are no laws that say you must hire the most qualified candidate for the job. Most employment laws attempt to define the ways in which a private sector company or manager can do the following:

- Establish job requirements (but not what they are)
- Interview applicants

- Make employment opportunities available
- Treat the employee on the job with respect to work hours and conditions, workplace safety, and certain other factors
- Terminate employment (in some states)

Laws also require companies to treat employees in certain ways, and they may regulate such factors as benefits packages and work hours. Depending on the industry, the company's size, and the amount of bureaucracy, these requirements may be more flexible or less flexible.

Write Clear Job Descriptions

In an ideal world, a written job description defines the basic expectations that you and your company have for employee performance. This message runs consistently through advertising, interviews, and performance evaluations. How closely reality matches the ideal varies widely; many small companies do not even have job descriptions because employees perform so many tasks that are essential to keeping the business running.

Beyond laws are corporate policies—the internal guidelines that tell managers what they can and cannot do when it comes to hiring, evaluating, promoting, and firing employees. It is always important to start by consulting with your HR department to make sure you are acting in a responsible manner from the perspective of the law and are complying with internal policies. Key questions to address include these:

- Must you interview and consider internal applicants before seeking external applicants?

- If internal applicants meet the job's basic requirements, must you hire them?
- Do union contracts include stipulations and procedures for considering potential employees?
- Do requirements differ for employees hired to fill vacated versus newly created positions?
- Do requirements differ according to the job's classification (hourly, salaried, exempt, nonexempt, permanent, temporary)?
- How can (or must) factors such as race and gender affect your selection process?
- Can you decide to hire someone with less experience or fewer qualifications because that person shows an eagerness and aptitude for learning, or must you accept the candidate whose actual skills are the strongest?
- Can you go through the entire interviewing process and decide that rather than hiring any of the candidates you want to post the job again?

The rules for jobs in the private sector differ from those in the public sector (government), those covered under union contracts and collective bargaining agreements, and in certain other settings. In such controlled settings, stringent details may regulate the entire process of hiring or promoting, placing any influence beyond your control.

THE JOB DESCRIPTION

Managers discuss the elements of the job description when they interview job applicants, so prospective employees will already know these actions will be among their responsibilities if or when they are hired. A job's specifications should be reasonable and realistic, yet they should also allow for expansion and growth as circumstances change within your company and the industry. Advances in technology might ratchet up expectations; it's important to communicate even in the job interview that employees need to stay ahead of the curve. When written correctly, the job description is the platform for the job's measurable standards. The more effectively you establish this in the job interview, the greater clarity new employees will have about your (and the company's) expectations.

Clarity and specific details should characterize all job descriptions, even if performance is difficult to quantify. Sometimes you need to take a step back to look beyond the apparent tasks of the job to assess what factors are within the employee's control. It's neither fair nor wise to hold people accountable for actions and results beyond their influence. Within the factors employees can control, identify and describe specific behaviors. For example, rather than expressing the general concept of "follow-up," identify the task instead: "Send thank-you notes to clients after projects are finished." This distinction makes clear the precise action you expect an employee to take and that you will measure.

When Possible, Recruit from Within

Many managers overlook the most highly qualified candidates: current employees. Even when companies routinely post jobs internally before conducting outside recruiting, managers may perceive the need to look outside the company. Taking an employee from another job leaves that department's manager looking for a replacement. But current employees have knowledge of the company and often have surprising skills and interests they don't use in their present jobs.

Ironically, many managers have little or nothing to do with writing descriptions for jobs in their departments. In many companies, the writing of job descriptions, and even the interviewing and hiring processes, are the venue of HR or personnel. This is often the case in companies that operate under collective bargaining agreements. It doesn't hurt, however, to offer your suggestions.

INTERVIEWING CANDIDATES

Can They Do the Job?

Job applications and resumes have a single purpose: to get the candidate an interview. It's asking for trouble to make an employment offer solely on the basis of written qualifications. You want to meet the person and have the opportunity to ask questions about his or her qualifications. Many people, particularly those who apply for technical or organizational jobs, have backgrounds and experiences that make for interesting conversation. There also is nothing like the "eyeball factor" to help you gauge how well someone might fit into the work group you supervise.

Lies in the Workplace

According to the *Wall Street Journal*, one-third of job candidates lie about their experience, education, or employment history on their applications or resumes. With alarming frequency the news media report stories of people caught in the lies of their resumes, from upper-level executives to college professors to research scientists.

But intuition is sometimes a faulty barometer. The sad truth is that more people than not lie on their resumes and on job applications. They may inflate their experience and qualifications or leave out less favorable details. Sometimes the misrepresentations have honorable intentions, such as the person who claims a college degree while still completing the last few credits. People may fudge employment dates to cover extended periods of unemployment, even when those periods occurred for reasons that would not harm their chances at future jobs.

Employment experts urge prospective employers to consistently check references to make sure at least the facts are correct. Many companies—and yours might be among them—are reluctant to do more than confirm dates of employment and job titles, but most will at least do that because such information is purely factual. Mismatches tell you that the person has either made a significant error or outright lied. Such actions are cause for immediate termination should the person make it past the hiring stage. When the lie is significant, it is difficult for it to escape detection for very long because the person's inability to perform the tasks will quickly become apparent.

INTERVIEW BASICS

The job interview is a two-way street. As you're trying to determine whether this person is a good fit for the job, the person you're interviewing is also evaluating those same factors. Though the pendulum swings along the job availability continuum, an applicant is no more likely to take your job, no questions asked, than you are to offer it.

The Perfect Candidate

Is the perfect candidate for your department's open position someone in another job in the company whose shoes would be hard to fill? Discuss transitional measures with the other manager. Sometimes passing over someone for a new position because the person is exceptionally good at his or her current job is enough to cause the person to leave for opportunities elsewhere. Better at least to keep this talent within your company.

The most effective approach is to structure the interview as a dialogue in which you ask a few questions about the candidate's experience or education, then let the candidate ask a few questions about the job and the work environment. Prospective employees want to know how you envision applying their skills and abilities; they will also be curious about the other employees in the department and what kinds of working relationships they might expect.

Some people may be most concerned with factors such as whether they can put family photos on their desks, while others want to know how you as the manager can separate the contributions multiple employees make to the same project. By the time the candidate reaches you for an interview, he or she has likely already made it through a preliminary interview with human resources. You may choose to offer a tour of the department or work area, or to introduce some of your key employees.

Finding the Right Match

Most jobs actually have two sets of requirements: those related to expertise and experience, and those related to personality and work style. Requirements related to skill sets appear to be fairly clear-cut and easy to establish. This is probably true for jobs in which the tasks are highly structured or even rote. If you need to hire someone to operate a punch press in the production department, it's easy enough to determine whether an applicant has the knowledge and skill to do this. Because the job itself is highly structured, the person's personality and work style are less relevant to performance. If you're hiring to fill a position in the sales department, the situation is far more subjective. Because the job involves forming relationships (however short-lived they might be), work style and personality are significant factors.

An Interview Example

There is more than one way to conduct an effective interview. Like Michael, you may employ a multilevel approach.

Michael was the manager of a software company's marketing department. His work group spent a lot of time together, and its productivity depended on how well employees could work collaboratively. It was crucial that new employees had both the appropriate job skills and the right "mesh" with the rest of the group. There was little room for frail egos or high-and-mighty attitudes, and Michael could sniff out either all the way from the lobby. His department needed people who were talented yet genuinely humble. They spent much of their time in meetings or on the phone with clients and prospective clients. They had to be people-people, and they had to be good listeners.

The company's HR department confirmed resumes and conducted preliminary interviews, then forwarded the applicants who met the job's technical qualifications and the company's basic requirements. One "test" Michael incorporated into job interviews was to drone on and on about a particular subject to see how the applicant responded. This gave him a sense of how the person might respond to a client who did the same thing. An applicant who maintained eye contact, nodded and smiled, and appeared to remain interested even when Michael began to bore himself earned an invitation to tour the department and meet with the group. An applicant who checked his watch, fidgeted in his chair, interrupted, or whose eyes glazed over was not likely to make it to the next round.

It was also important to Michael that the people he hired have diverse interests. His department supported a wide range of clients and projects. So he also engaged applicants in dialogue about events in the news. He broached topics of interest to the local community, to see whether an applicant could pick up the threads and weave them into a conversation. And he asked both work-related and more general-interest questions, just to see how he felt as he and the applicant talked. At this point, intuition guided many of Michael's reactions. Was this a person he wanted to spend time around? Was this someone he wanted to mentor or nurture? Was this someone who would get along well with the department's current employees and clients?

The final step in Michael's hiring process was to have the applicant meet with a number of his employees. He usually scheduled a formal meeting in which three to five employees sat down with the applicant to describe their work and ask the applicant questions. Michael also tried to have several informal connections take place, to get "first impression" feedback from employees as well.

Before making a final decision, he reviewed all the factors, and compared them to what he knew were his personal biases. One of those biases was about attitude. Michael felt it was nearly always a better decision to hire someone who was eager and cooperative but a little short on practical experience than someone whose experience was astounding but who had an arrogant attitude. When Michael was satisfied that he had a balanced and quantifiable perspective, he consulted with HR one last time and then made a decision.

There are aspects of Michael's approach that appear arbitrary. It encompasses intangibles, such as his ability to select employees that his experience tells him are good choices. These are inherent dimensions of subjective judgment. But if you look closely, you'll see that Michael's approach incorporates a great deal of consistency as well, one that follows the same pattern of questioning in each interview.

THE INTERVIEW FROM START TO FINISH

Hiring the Best

Interviewing is a craft. You won't excel at it right away, but you can become quite skilled as your experience grows. There are many books and workshops that focus specifically on interviewing; if your job involves more than one or two interviews a year, invest in some training. At the very least, take an HR specialist or manager to lunch and ask for tips and suggestions. In general, in your interview you should do the following:

- Describe the actual job activities. Explain what a typical day in your department is like and what kinds of successes and challenges employees encounter.
- Describe the work environment. Is it collaborative or independent? Do people get individual recognition, or does the group sink or swim as one? Is there a lot of overtime, and what compensation is there, if any, for putting in extra hours?
- Ask a few questions that require simple, factual responses about information on the resume or job application. Watch for hesitancy in responding or for answers that don't match what's on paper.
- Ask the applicant for examples that demonstrate his or her abilities and skills in particular areas. If building relationships with prospective clients is important to the job, ask the applicant to describe two or three similar experiences that relate to your circumstances.

- Press for specifics. If an applicant says, "I like that kind of environment," ask how it is similar to or differs from work environments the employee has experienced in the past. If the employee says he or she has done "something like that," get details. Just how, exactly, was the applicant's previous experience "like" the requirements of the job?
- Listen for grandiose claims or statements that don't make sense. If in doubt, question. Again, press for specifics and ask for examples. Back-pedaling and convoluted explanations should raise the red flag about the candidate.

Keep your comments neutral and your thoughts to yourself. Unless you know without a doubt that this is the person you intend to hire, don't give the impression that this is the case. Likewise, don't imply that you're not hiring this person, either. No deal is a done deal until the hired candidate shows up for work. It's worth your while to remain open and positive with candidates who come in second or third. You may be able to go back to them when other jobs become available or if your first choice washes out for any reason. Some human resources experts estimate that as many as a third of new hires do not stay in their new jobs.

MAINTAINING BALANCE

The challenge for all managers is to balance the book and the story. The book—laws, regulations, policies—follows a strict structure. The story—personalities, work styles, potential—exists within and at the same time extends beyond the book. While it's crucial for you to go by the book as far as laws and company policies go, it's also essential for you to make decisions that are consistent with the story of your department (its needs). There has to be a happy medium between finding the best person to advance the interests of the company and finding a person who will best fit with the group.

This isn't to say that you should only hire people you like or that your employees must approve of new members to the team. Not all jobs require close interaction among employees. Use sound and rational judgment. It's more important for a computer programmer to know your company's network and applications inside and out than it is for that candidate to be able to discuss the political environment in the Middle East. It might even be acceptable for this person to be a bit on the antisocial side—computers don't engage in dialogue— as long as he or she has the right technical skills and isn't toxic to others. You might not want to go for coffee with this employee, but he or she will nonetheless make a positive contribution to your department or company.

PLAY IT SAFE

There are a lot of topics you cannot ask about in an interview. Among the obvious should be age and religion. Also high on the taboo list are birthplace, marital status, children, sexual orientation, or anything that might allow you (intentionally or unintentionally) to make a judgment based on class, background, lifestyle, or other factors not related to the job's requirements. Be sure you discuss all of these factors with your HR representative and understand, fully and completely, your legal obligations. Failing to do so can have serious consequences for you personally as well as for your company.

If the employment process truly were as simple as following all the laws and rules, there would be no need for employment attorneys. But employment law is a growing field, which tells us that laws and policies aren't enough. Jobs are about more than skill sets. Jobs are about the people who fill them, no matter how much companies might want to diminish that factor.

CONCLUDING THE INTERVIEW

When it's time to conclude the job interview, let the candidate know what to expect—when he or she might next hear from you, your timeline for filling the position, and whether to anticipate another round of interviews. Some managers like to ask the person for any final thoughts or questions. Although you might be ready to extend a job offer or decline the candidate at the conclusion of the interview, you would be wise to assess all the candidates a final time before making any decisions. Moreover, it is especially difficult to say, "Thanks, but no" in person to someone who hopes to get the job.

REFERENCE CHECKS

No matter how good a candidate appears on paper and in an interview, an important final step in the hiring process is to check references. Many companies have waiver forms for prospective employees to sign that grant them permission to contact references. Most references, especially former employers, will not even confirm employment without such a form. When contacting references, focus on verifying the facts the candidate put on the job application. Ask the reference source to provide details: "When did Stacy work for you, and what positions did she hold?"

Question discrepancies with care; this is often a road worth traveling only when the candidate is at the top of your list. Listen for carefully worded responses. Sometimes you learn more from what people *don't* tell you. As during your interview with the applicant, refrain from asking personal or lifestyle questions such as those about marital status, health concerns, or children. Not only is this information none of your business, it's also against the law to consider such factors when making job or promotion decisions.

LANDING THE NEW WORKER

You've made your choice, and now it's time to close the deal. Most managers first telephone the person to extend the job offer, and then follow up with a written letter to confirm. You're enthusiastic and excited to welcome this person aboard, so let it show! Though in some situations the job offer is a process of negotiation, most often the candidate knows the terms of employment. Nonetheless, you should review them in your phone conversation.

Some people, especially those who work in technical or competitive fields, have applied for multiple jobs and may be considering several offers. Other people may want to take some time to think about working for you and your company. Extend a time period for the person to consider your offer—forty-eight hours is reasonable. Call back after that time. If the person accepts, send the confirmation letter by mail (return receipt requested or certified mail is a good idea).

What if your chosen candidate declines your offer? Thank the candidate for his or her time, hang up the phone, and move on to your second choice. After an interview, people can change their minds or become uninterested for any number of reasons. Some will contact you to take themselves out of contention, though most will wait to see whether you offer a job. In circumstances when the candidate was someone who seemed very enthusiastic during the interview, you might ask the reason for the change of heart. You might discover factors you didn't consider or circumstances about the job that the candidate misinterpreted. You may have a chance to encourage your top choice to reconsider if you feel he or she is highly qualified and desirable for the job.

LAYOFFS

Dealing with the Hard Times

Things change: company leadership or ownership, market share, technology, regulations affecting particular industries, people. As a result, departments and sometimes even entire companies consolidate, combining resources in attempts to get more with less. Such changes often affect people across the company through no actions of their own. In other circumstances, people instigate change themselves through poor job performance or disciplinary issues the company can resolve only by severing ties. Sometimes hiring or promoting a person was a mistake. In nearly any scenario of change, managers shoulder the burden of swinging the axe and cleaning up afterward.

WHEN YOU'RE THE BEARER OF BAD NEWS

Although it's difficult to be the bearer of bad news, laying off employees doesn't have to be a nightmare you relive over and over. There will be challenges, and there may be reverberating effects of layoffs and downsizing, but you'll only prove your strengths as a manager if you handle the situation gracefully. For example, let's consider what Rosalyn did.

Rosalyn learned in September that her company would reduce its workforce by 30 percent in February. As a manager, Rosalyn had to assess her staff to determine how the skills and strengths of each employee would fit within the new structure. These assessments would determine who would stay and who would be let go. Knowing so far in advance also gave Rosalyn time to think through her decisions and frame the decidedly negative situation in the most supportive way possible.

When the day finally arrived for Rosalyn to issue pink slips, people were understandably upset—even those who didn't lose their jobs. Rosalyn talked individually with each employee being laid off, explaining that it was purely economics and had nothing to do with performance. Even so, the employees, both surviving and laid off, felt the company and Rosalyn, their manager, had betrayed them.

After the laid-off employees left, Rosalyn called a meeting with the survivors. She explained that she understood and accepted their perceptions of the situation but wanted the opportunity to explain her actions. She told each remaining employee that she was very sorry to see each laid-off employee leave, but there had been no choice about cutbacks if the company itself was going to survive.

Then Rosalyn pulled out some charts and reports and started talking about the company's economic status. She showed employees what the company had to produce in terms of billable days just to cover operating costs and make a minimal profit. Everyone was surprised at what it took to keep the company running. The meeting gave them a greater understanding of the challenges the company faced and also an appreciation for the careful way in which the company had approached the downsizing.

Another dimension of the downsizing was restructuring. Several other departments that had also laid off employees were consolidating, which meant Rosalyn's department was gaining employees and functions from other parts of the company.

Rosalyn discussed how these employees would fit into the department and allowed her employees to help decide how to reorganize the department to accommodate them. Rosalyn concluded the meeting by thanking the employees for the good work they'd done and expressing her confidence that their strong performance would continue.

Rosalyn handled a bad situation with grace and honesty. Everyone could see that though the situation was beyond individual control, Rosalyn made informed decisions that matched the company's changing needs with the abilities of the employees in her department. Though everyone was angry about the situation, they could not fault Rosalyn for the way she handled it. As a manager, you will undoubtedly face such unpleasant challenges yourself. No one likes shattering another person's world. But everyone has the capacity to handle such a task with professionalism and compassion, as Rosalyn did.

BIG PICTURE: RESTRUCTURING AND DOWNSIZING

Companies restructure or downsize to conserve resources and cut expenses, and they generally do this because their share of the marketplace has become viciously competitive and there's no longer any way to stay profitable without significant changes. (Restructuring nearly always means downsizing in some way.) Sometimes these are desperation measures made in an attempt to pull the company back from the brink of bankruptcy or closure. While an acquisition or a merger generally has benefits for both companies, individual workers pay the price. Some jobs *will* disappear when your company or even only your department merges with another.

Restructuring and Downsizing

As a manager, you have to be ready to meet the demands of restructuring and downsizing in two ways. First, you need to prepare your employees and support the company by making the changes work. Second, you have to protect your own career.

Restructuring and downsizing have become more the rule than the exception in today's business world. Industries change rapidly, technology changes rapidly, and companies across industries have learned that survival means being nimble. Companies must meet opportunities and demands, and employees must be ready to be shaken up along the way. Even stodgy industries like insurance are changing seemingly overnight. New consumer trends mean new expectations for all kinds of products and services, from computers to life insurance.

Open the Channels of Communication

Communication is critical in times of challenge. As much as possible (and only when the company is making the information available to employees), managers should try to let people know what actions the company is considering and how these actions might affect individual workers. As a downsized or restructured department moves forward, it's important for the manager to be sensitive to workflow, personality conflicts, confusion over who does what, and potential problems.

The restructured group might perceive its manager as somewhat of a stepparent who has partiality toward his or her original employees. If you are this manager, you might feel damned if you do, damned if you don't. Employees are likely to accuse you (or, less personally, the company) of overworking them to increase profits. Sometimes there is a grain of truth in this perception; the company wouldn't have downsized in the first place if it could support all of its resources. Doing more with less, whether equipment or people, is both a challenge and a goal.

Protect Yourself

Major changes in your company will undoubtedly lead you to reconsider your own career. Although you must be cheerleader, mediator, parent, and coach for your employees, you might not believe in the company's new direction. When departments are restructured, managers are sometimes among the first to go as the company attempts to shave costs by retaining the people who actually do the work. You need to be ready to move within the company or to another company. This is the reality of the marketplace.

Companies want loyalty, but at the same time they expect us all to accept change and be ready to move. They are not there to provide us security for life. You need to keep your professional skills current. Stay abreast of current thinking and technology, both in your field and in general. These are the factors that will help you make a move when you need to. There is nothing sadder than a person with twenty years in at the Big Corporation who knows nothing beyond how to survive at the Big Corporation.

FIRING AN EMPLOYEE

When Things Just Don't Work Out

No manager enjoys the prospect of firing an employee. Firing someone is the most serious consequence for failing to improve. Before you come to the decision that you need to end a person's employment, you must be sure in your heart of hearts that this is the right thing to do. Then you must make certain that you have complied with any and all relevant laws, regulations, and company policies and that all of the paperwork is completely in order. Laws may regulate employee actions such as firing in your state. Most companies further establish strict policies that require extensive documentation affirming that you have followed those policies. Work closely with your HR department, if your company has one, to be sure you do things right—for your sake as well as the employee's. This is a decision from which there is no turning back.

"Work at Will"

Most private sector (nongovernment) jobs are "work at will" positions in which the employee works at the will (and sometimes whimsy) of the employer. Though most mid-size to large companies have specific "fire for cause" policies and terms of employment, these protections are not as yet required by law. In "work at will" states, companies do not need reasons to fire employees, though federal discrimination laws may apply in some circumstances.

The decisions you make regarding an employee's job status—to promote or not, to give a raise or not, to fire or keep on—are not decisions to make without careful deliberation. Plan the meeting to fire the employee according to your company's policies and procedures. Some managers prefer to conduct a firing at the end of the workday, so the employee can collect his or her things and leave without everyone else watching. Will a security guard have to escort the fired employee back to the office to gather his or her possessions and then out of the building? Do you or an HR representative need to supervise the packing?

As humiliating as such requirements might seem, they are often necessary safeguards for the company to prevent theft or sabotage. If the employee has valued work saved on the company's computer network or on a company computer, back up all the files the night before you intend to fire the employee as an added protection. Before the meeting, rehearse what you intend to say. Practice speaking clearly and unemotionally. When you do meet with the employee, take the following steps:

- Have an HR representative or your boss present as well. This bolsters your authority and lessens the likelihood of emotional pleas or outbursts.
- If your company policies or employment agreements allow the employee to have a representative present, make sure the scheduled meeting accommodates this.
- Keep the conversation short, to the point, and unemotional.
- Review the conversations and documentation that support the decision to fire the employee.

In this meeting, it is not necessary or advisable to invite the employee's comments or perspective. The time for that is long past. If you've done your job as a manager, the firing shouldn't come as a total shock to the employee (although the finality of it might be temporarily stunning). You've counseled the employee about his or her performance issues or whatever problems have led to this point, and you've given the employee plenty of opportunities to fix the problems. Keep your cool and stick with the script you've rehearsed. If it is necessary for someone to escort the fired employee from the premises, be sure that person is ready and waiting.

Follow the Rules

Union contracts, collective bargaining agreements, and other binding pacts may stipulate the conditions and procedures for firing an employee. It is essential to follow such stipulations to protect yourself and your company from legal action down the road.

As soon as possible after the terminated employee has gone, assemble the other members of the team to give them the news. Keep the reasons for the employee's termination to yourself; such information is confidential. It's important to treat people with respect after they've been fired, regardless of the reasons for firing them. Chances are, the other team members knew this was coming, and it is likely they know better than you do why this was the only option. Sometimes, however, you need to reassure other employees that this was a matter specific to the fired employee; it's natural for them to feel some fear and apprehension about the security of their own jobs.

Other employees may want to talk about how they feel, but it's generally better to focus on how duties will be reassigned, what the plans are for hiring a replacement, and other such work-related details. The key is to move on. Those who remain will watch how you handle things, and their perceptions will affect their attitudes, performance, and loyalty.

HANDLING THE FALLOUT WITH OTHER EMPLOYEES

The problems and performance issues of a coworker often affect other employees, sometimes deeply, and they often arise well before you make the decision to fire the employee. No matter how swiftly you might have moved to intervene, they probably think it took too long. And if it did take you a while to catch on to the reality of the situation, other employees are likely to be frustrated and resentful. They may retaliate by deliberately dragging out timelines, refusing to do anything beyond the minimum required of them, or quitting. Leaving problems to fester is like a poison that sickens the entire work group and can permanently damage the team's cohesiveness and collaborative spirit. Ultimately the situation reflects poorly on you as well; managers stand or fall based on the effectiveness and productivity of their employees.

If this fallout is a big deal—the company loses a major account or other departments become involved—consider holding a team meeting. You must discover to what extent the fired employee disrupted the performance of the other employees who themselves perhaps couldn't complete their assignments or had to watch their efforts go to waste.

For this team meeting, deliberately plan the direction you want to take it and the comments you wish to make. Meet in a location where you and the work group can speak candidly and without being overheard. Establish parameters and limits from the start: no bashing, no gossip. Explain that you know about the problems, and that you are working to establish an improvement plan that includes measures for follow-up. Then invite the other employees to share their concerns. Keep the conversation focused on processes and outcomes—don't let the discussion stray to people and personalities. A certain amount of venting is inevitable, but strive to keep the tone from turning belligerent or derogatory.

Confidentiality Is the Best Policy

It is inappropriate and often illegal for you to discuss one employee's difficulties with other employees. Given that performance problems affect the entire team, it's probable that the work group has become a part of those difficulties. Nonetheless, you must still keep the fired employee's difficulties in strict confidence.

It's important for other employees to understand that you know and care about how the problems have affected them and their work. As much as they might be concerned for their now-former coworker, they also need reassurance that their performance is fine and their jobs are safe. Most people are compassionate and forgiving; if they see that you have responded thoroughly and fairly, the work group will support your efforts. Crisis often causes groups to pull together or fall apart; if yours is a cohesive and well-functioning group, it will rally. If trust and confidence within the work group is severely damaged, however, it might take considerable time for the wounds to heal and the group to return to full function.

PERSONAL ACCOUNTABILITY

The Buck Stops Here

Managers are accountable on several fronts for their performances in the workplace: their bosses, their employees, the company, and the various laws and regulations that apply. In some situations such accountability can take a very personal turn, such as when someone names you as party to a legal action or your conduct violates the law. Regulations hold companies accountable for compliance; companies similarly hold their managers accountable. Your company certainly expects your actions to remain within its policies; step outside the boundaries, and you could find yourself standing in the unemployment line.

Treat People As Individuals

Consistency and realistic latitude should coexist in company policies. There are times when following the rules to the letter is counterproductive. Granting exceptions demonstrates an understanding that individuals sometimes have differing needs. Establish a process for considering exceptions that looks at the specific circumstances, the benefits for the employee, and the benefits for the company. If you decide to deviate from policy, explain your reasons for making the decision and emphasize that this is an exception, not a new way of interpreting the policy.

As a manager, you have your own accountability to consider as well as the accountability of the employees who report to you. It is part of your role to make sure everyone understands the laws, regulations, policies, and practices that apply to them and the conduct of their jobs. You may have formal responsibility for arranging or conducting in-service training and other educational processes to familiarize the employees who report to you with relevant health and safety regulations and practices. When you encounter questionable practices or circumstances, question them. This encourages employees to do the same. And when employees bring concerns to you, take prompt action to investigate them.

THE OPEN DOOR POLICY

The open door is both literal and symbolic. If you tell employees they can come to talk with you anytime but you work with your door closed, you are sending a mixed message. Most people see closed doors as stop signs. From childhood, we're trained not to enter without knocking, and we often hesitate to knock unless the need to talk to the person on the other side can't wait. Sometimes managers close doors out of habit or to block distractions. But are you blocking out distractions or are you blocking out others who might see or hear what you're doing? And what constitutes a distraction? Conversations? People walking past? The noises of a busy work group? Ringing telephones? An employee's question? It's difficult to define clear guidelines. Even if you truly want people to just open the door and come in, many will be reluctant to do so. Unless you're working on something that requires privacy, leave your door open. The only way people know you have an open-door policy is if your door truly is open. Consider the following example.

When Mark became manager of the assembly group, he established what he believed was an effective open-door policy. He would see any employee about any matter—as long as the employee scheduled an appointment through his secretary and could provide evidence that he or she had tried to resolve the concern through what Mark called "first-level intervention." If the problem was about taking leave time, for example, the employee first needed to talk with the other employee who had already scheduled time off to see if the two of them could negotiate a compromise or with HR if the issue was policy- or benefits-related.

At first, employees welcomed Mark's approach. The group's previous manager only talked to people who were in some sort of trouble and kept group meetings focused on discussions of work tasks. In contrast, Mark seemed amazingly open. Within the first few months, every employee had scheduled an appointment to talk with Mark. While he was friendly enough in these one-on-one meetings, he kept them just as focused as the previous manager had kept group meetings. When an employee came to Mark's office for a scheduled appointment, Mark expected the employee to present a one- to three-minute summary of the problem and the steps the employee had taken to attempt to resolve it. He had little interest in casual conversation, and no interest in matters that weren't directly related to work processes or results.

When employees had problems they felt needed immediate intervention, Mark was again friendly but firm. He was happy to do what he could to help, but asked them to please schedule an appointment to discuss the situation.

Not surprisingly, appointments soon dropped off. Mark interpreted this as an indication that the group had finally come together as a smoothly functioning team capable of troubleshooting and problem solving on its own. But the employees grew increasingly dissatisfied. At least their previous manager had made it unmistakably clear that she had no interest in them and their problems. Mark gave all the appearances of being interested, but in the end he was no more approachable than the previous manager. Requiring appointments to see Mark meant that his "open" door was shut tight to employees unless their needs fit into Mark's schedule. Although Mark believed he was available, his rules and procedures made him inaccessible.

THE FEEDBACK LOOP

"Feedback" is a sort of buzzword that has different meanings depending on the context. In electronics, feedback is undesirable sound distortion. In the workplace, feedback is one person giving another person a reaction or response—which sometimes sounds like the annoying whines and screeches we associate with electronic feedback. In communication, feedback all too often becomes synonymous with criticism. When a manager says, "I have some feedback for you," employees often hear, "Let me tell you how you screwed up—again!"

Under ideal circumstances, feedback is a loop, a cycle of action and reaction. Neither component needs to be big or significant. In fact, when feedback becomes a communication loop, most people don't notice that it's even taking place. It's when feedback is absent, negative, or devastating that it garners any attention. Of course not all feedback is positive, and sometimes it is downright devastating. But on the feedback continuum, most should fall somewhere in the center.

The Manager's View

Employees always want to know how their managers view them and their work. It's human nature; we are creatures of response. We want to know what others think of us. It helps us to develop a sense of belonging (or not), accomplishment (or not), and confidence (or not). People constantly seek feedback from their managers. Some ask for it directly: "How did I do?" Others are less direct: "What did the client say?" Although conventional wisdom preaches that no news is good news, in the corporate world the reverse is more often the case. Or at least that's what employees think, as they fret and worry because they haven't heard anything from you.

Some feedback should take place in public, such as in a meeting. Take a few minutes to acknowledge an employee who has done an exceptional job. This makes the employee feel good; recognition in front of peers is the highest compliment. It also solidifies roles and responsibilities, and it shapes interaction within the group. People feel affirmed for their contributions.

Offer Compliments

To balance your limited time with an employee's high level of need for feedback, try breaking your comments into smaller bites. Instead of waiting until an assignment is completed to congratulate the employee on a job well done, offer compliments and suggestions along the way.

Fairness and appropriateness are critical, of course; it's important that you avoid giving the impression of playing favorites. Public praise can backfire if it makes other employees feel less significant. Private feedback also has its place. Stop by an employee's workstation to offer congratulations on a report well written or a project completed ahead of schedule. This individual attention shows that you notice and care about individual effort.

Feedback to Help Employees Grow

Feedback is a great way to regularly provide tips and suggestions to help employees improve and grow their skills. Given regularly and in small bits, such feedback quickly becomes a natural element of the work environment, and people come to expect it. Consistency and frequency of delivery removes any sense of discipline or heavy-handedness from the feedback process. Furthermore, you should not sugarcoat feedback; most people resent attempts to cloak bad news in the trappings of compliments.

Comment on specific actions and behaviors. "Barb was very upset that you yelled at her about the delay at the print shop, and that you hung up on her" works better than "Johnson, you're an insensitive boor!" Whenever practical, give feedback that is specific yet offers choices. "In reading this report, I didn't get a sense of what the product actually is. Would you please restructure the introduction or add another section to part two?"

Look for ways to frame less-than-positive feedback in the context of realistic improvement. "Customer complaints about delivery delays are up 35 percent this quarter. Let's take a look at the reasons for the delays and then brainstorm some solutions."

As much as possible, praise the entire work group for its collective efforts. This reinforces the team's value and reminds people that teamwork is about performance, not about personalities or stroking egos.

Some managers want to be good guys so they give only positive feedback, and this at the drop of a hat. It doesn't take long for employees to figure out that praise is always forthcoming, which diminishes its value. And when feedback that was initially positive is followed by a contradictory message, then the feedback becomes even less valuable. If the news is bad, just deliver it. These people are adults; they know, even if you attempt to hide it from them, that they make mistakes and that life is not all roses and chocolate. When less-than-positive feedback involves just one or two people, deliver it individually and in private. When the message is for the entire group, be direct but compassionate. Don't single out individuals in the group setting; if you have additional specific comments, deliver them in private.

INDEX